DEEP PURPLE

A Matter Of Fact

Jerry Bloom

First published in USA in 2015
by Wymer Publishing
Bedford, England
www.wymerpublishing.co.uk
Tel: 01234 326691
Wymer Publishing is a trading name of Wymer (UK) Ltd

ISBN 978-1-908724-06-9

Proofreading by Lynn Baker.

Typeset by Wymer.
Printed and bound by
Lightning Source, USA

A catalogue record for this book is available from the British Library.

Cover design by Wymer.

DEEP PURPLE

A Matter Of Fact

Jerry Bloom

WP
WYMER
PUBLISHING
Bedford, England

CONTENTS

Foreword

Deep Purple came in to my life as a teenager. I had seen *Made In Japan* in my brother's bedroom alongside *Physical Graffiti*, Lou Reed's *Transformer*, The Stones *Sticky Fingers* and other such classics, though to be fair I hadn't paid it much attention until I discovered rock, and what a discovery it was! Making a tape from the record and playing it to death on my cassette Walkman. This came in very handy whilst travelling from Australia on 40 hour plus journeys to reach junior tennis tournaments around the world in the late seventies.

To this day I can recall every single note of *Made In Japan*, every ad-lib and comment and I steal Ian Gillan's "I want everything louder than everything else" comment regularly to this day. I'm not the only one who knows the album inside out. At one *Sunflower* charity concert in 2013 Jacky Paice, the lovely wife of Ian, and I watched with amusement as Iron Maiden singer Bruce Dickinson got up with Deep Purple and co. and sang with Ian Gillan and ad-libbed word perfect from the album.

As I travelled I'd pick up more albums, often terrible 4th or 5th generation tape to tape recordings from Hong Kong or elsewhere but I didn't care. Deep Purple were the most original thing I had ever heard and it would be hard to argue that 'Child in Time' wasn't the most incredibly creative full guitar based rock 'n' roll thing fans had ever heard. It blew my mind back then and still does today.

This book of short stories come from the very early days on the UK circuit all the way through to the present day and will shine some light on the ups and downs of one of the most influential and popular rock bands of all time. Most Deep Purple fans will be aware of the story behind 'Smoke On The Water' but there is plenty of misconception around the members. Jerry Bloom does an amazing job of collecting a collage of information and stories of the band members when they were in and out of their various bands before, during and after Purple. The stories will keep any Deep Purple fan enthralled. As anyone in showbiz will tell you there's always a whole lot more going on than it appears.

This book is not just about the rock 'n' roll lifestyle but an insight in to the tough day to day grind of a group of amazingly talented artists all with differing personalities. It's easy to forget that Deep Purple along with Led Zeppelin and Black Sabbath were not only trail blazing a new style of rock but a new path for many a touring band for the future, often with hilarious repercussions.

Deep Purple has influenced many people's lives, but few can say that they have had a major physical effect as they have on me. Well to be precise

Ian Gillan. Not long after becoming Wimbledon singles champion I broke my Achilles tendon and was sidelined for many months. As mentioned in one of the stories, I met Ian through a mutual friend, charity campaigner Jon Dee not long after they had put together the all star 'Smoke On The Water' remake.

I invited Ian to the pre-Wimbledon tournament at Queens Club in South West London for an afternoon of top tennis. Earlier in the day I had a meeting in the West End of London and had booked a cab to get back. Well as often happens in London an underground tube strike was under way and there was no movement in the traffic at all. I decided to get out and walk, after my wife had informed me that Ian was waiting in my front room to go to the tennis. Not wanting to leave my idol waiting I decided to walk, well limp home as I was barely off crutches. As it turned out, the 5 or so miles slog back home to greet Ian has given me a permanent limp! One that I still get comments on now more than 25 years later. When I hear Ian's chilling scream in 'Speed King' I always have a little grin on my face. That was a day I was certainly anything but a speed king.

Pat Cash, November 2014

Preface

There haven't been a huge amount of books written on Deep Purple but the band continues to draw enormous interest around the world that encourages much discussion amongst fans. Since the advent of the Internet many websites have provided a lot of material about the band and in more recent times, social media has created a platform for discussions.

Whilst these sources have made a great deal of additional information freely available, one habit that continues to plague these modern forms of communication is the propensity for cut and paste. If a fact is wrong on one website it doesn't take long before it has spread like wildfire around the World Wide Web.

The number of websites that claim Ritchie Blackmore's middle name is Harold, that the band was formed in Hertford or still refer to Purple as the loudest band in the world are just some examples of many things that are still being taken as gospel. And through the mists of time, even the band has relayed past events incorrectly. As examples, in 1989 when talking about the hassles involved in recording *Machine Head*, Jon Lord said they originally started it at the Conference Centre in Montreux. Not so, that was where *Burn* was recorded. And as for Ian Paice and David Coverdale's misleading comments on run-ins with one of the support bands at the Sunbury Festival in 1975, that will be elaborated upon further on in this book.

Rather than present factual information in a standard biographical format, I have tried a new approach of short stories and anecdotes on specific events or connections that have been a part of Purple's long and illustrious history; the sort of things that many fans will have questioned. I have also taken an offbeat and fun approach with some of the stories by presenting them with a look at various people and events that in some way or another are linked to the band. And whilst they all include factual information I have often presented them in a more light-hearted way.

The information has come from several sources including various band members; the files of the original management company and the author's own first hand observations. The main remit is to produce a book that is squarely aimed at the more casual fan and will hopefully clarify facts surrounding several stories that have been incorrectly regaled throughout the years. But it also unearths information that should even be new to the most diehard Purple devotees. The end result should hopefully be seen for what it is - a fun read that also sheds plenty of new light to the various shades of Deep Purple. Enjoy.

Before Deep Purple
there was... Deep Purple!

As the MI5, Ian Paice and Rod Evans' pre-Purple band had a promising start. They were signed to *EMI's Parlophone* label in 1966 and released one single. Later that year the band changed its name to The Maze and signed to Robert Stigwood's *Reaction* label and recorded and released another single.

Early 1967 saw them touring Germany followed by a three-month stint in Italy. Back in England, Saturday 8 July, The Maze had a gig at Great Yarmouth's Floral Hall, which hosted bands every Wednesday and Saturday. An advert in the *Eastern Evening News* the previous day listed forthcoming bands appearing: *On Wednesday 12th it was P.P. Arnold and The Nice, and the following Wednesday, The Pink Floyd.* But before that, the Saturday night gig by the Maze, "recording for *Reaction*", also listed the support band... THE DEEP PURPLE!

History has previously documented the idea for Deep Purple's name coming from Blackmore. All the guys have publicly gone on record saying that they chose the name from the 1933 song, reportedly a favourite of Ritchie's grandma, which had been a hit for several acts, the most recent having been by Nino Tempo & April Stevens in 1963.

"It was a song my grandmother used to play on the piano. I once saw it in print that it was the last song she ever played - but I don't think it was. She just tinkered around on the piano - but she used to play 'Deep Purple'," says Blackmore.

But this support band at Paice and Evans' gig a few months before "the" Deep Purple was formed shines a different light on the matter. Could Paice or Evans have casually mentioned the name of that group during those early days at Deeves Hall in March 1968 or was it pure coincidence?

Little is known about this Deep Purple and it is also unclear whether or not the band was still going when our Deep Purple signed to *Parlophone* and *Tetragrammaton* in early 1968. Conventional wisdom suggests it was a Norfolk band. A book on famous Norwich landmarks lists Deep Purple as playing the Orford Cellar, a popular club for emerging bands in the sixties, where Cream and Hendrix performed. It mistakenly took it to be "the" Deep Purple; although the only time they played in Norwich was two nights on the

Burn tour in 1974. This band was probably only around for a few months in '67 and could well have disbanded before Blackmore, Lord, Paice, Evans and Simper took hold of the name, but might still have been in action in early '68.

And if that wasn't enough, Mike Wheeler who used the stage surname, Dee (and was bandleader of the Jaywalkers, Blackmore's first professional band in 1961) was in a short-lived band called Deep Purple formed around late October 1967, immediately after his band The All Night Workers split. This Deep Purple certainly took its name from the pre-wartime song that Mick Wheeler's mother used to sing in her husband's band. Wheeler remembers his version playing a few shows, but by February 1968 the band had split up.

To muddy the waters further several gigs were played by Deep Purple in the South Coast region in early '68 including one gig at a venue called the Cobweb in Brighton in early April. But it wasn't Wheeler's band, the Norfolk band, or indeed the Purple that had just got together in Deeves Hall in Hertfordshire.

Unbelievably this was yet another Deep Purple, who hailed from Hastings. The band's former manager Mick O'Dowd confirmed this in the *Hastings Observer* on 2 May 2014: "I was Deep Purple's

manger for a time and they were previously called The Likes Of Us. It shows that we had the name before the other lot as the local group were gigging while the nucleus of the others were in Episode Six and in fact played the Cobweb after Deep Purple. Hastings has always been a hotbed of topline groups and artists appearing at the Pier, Witchdoctor, Cobweb and Aquarius clubs, to name but a few, over the years. Bowie often played at The Witchdoctor and Cobweb and Ronnie Wood played with The Birds there."

[Photo: John M. Sheppard]

One of the newest pop groups to hit the local 'scene' are five boys who call themselves 'The Deep Purple,' and who have had engagements in East Sussex and Kent for about four months now.

Specialising in the highly popular 'soul' and 'tamla Motown' sounds, and judging from

to be playing at the 'Witch Doctor'—to be re-named 'The Cobweb'—when it opens.

Seen in the picture is 'The Deep Purple'—from left to right: Peter Horton (lead guitarist), Tony Bird (organ and flute), Ian McGilvray (drums), Len Benton (bass

guitar)' and the younges member of the group 17-yea old Tich Turner (lead vocal, Road Manager Brian Bern says that the group have 'go the voices and the sound' t needed a good Recordin Manager. Are there an offers?

Come what may, with no fewer than three other Deep Purples on the scene in late '67 and early '68, despite the popularity of the song of the same name, it's possible that either Paice or Evans had it kicking around in their sub-consciousness when the various names were discussed at Deeves Hall before the band set sail for their first gigs in Denmark. It certainly adds another slant on the possibility of why they chose the name.

In The Beginning...

Although the first Deep Purple was Blackmore, Lord, Paice, Evans and Simper, several other names were bandied about before settling upon the line-up that scored a US hit with its debut single 'Hush'.

It is well documented that ex-Searcher's drummer Chris Curtis was the initial catalyst for the band, with his vision of a musical roundabout. Curtis had put the seeds in motion in late 1967, having enticed Tony Edwards of the clothing company *Alice Edwards Holdings Ltd* to invest in a new band.

However this brief period before the completed line-up finally emerged is somewhat murky. Firstly Curtis encountered Jon Lord at a party. The organist was at that time in the live backing band for The Flowerpot Men. Curtis then told Lord about Ritchie Blackmore, a sensational guitarist he knew who was living in Hamburg. "I was in Hamburg and had played with The Searchers in 1963, and remained friends with Chris Curtis", Blackmore later recalled, although his comment is slightly misleading. Blackmore did not actually play with The Searchers but on the same bill.

The Searchers were in Hamburg from 30th April to 17th June 1963. Blackmore at the time was in The Outlaws who were the backing band for Jerry Lee Lewis at Hamburg's famous Star Club on May 13th, 15th-19th. In an interview published as *Man Of Mystery* in *Sounds*, February 8 1975, Blackmore said: "I was there in 1966 and '67, living off of immoral earnings. I've lived over there quite a few times, once in 1963 right after The Beatles were there. I did the rounds then as well, it was a great time then. There was eight bands a night in the Star Club. And they had this programme worked out; a band would play for an hour and then come off. There were some great people around then - Tony Sheridan who is a great singer - Ray Charles. I was with Jerry Lee Lewis, Gene Vincent; The Searchers were on."

Back to '67 and Blackmore returned to England, but was unimpressed with Chris Curtis's vision of a roundabout approach with a nucleus of musicians, whilst others could jump on and off at any time! "Nothing happened. I was waiting to join but nothing happened," explains Blackmore. "I had remained friends with Chris Curtis. When he wanted to put a band together he sent me all these telegrams in Hamburg and called me over. He was very animated and very theatrical. 'Who's in the band? What's the deal?' And he would go: 'the best guitarist in the world is you. You're in the band: You'll be playing second guitar'. 'So you'll be playing lead, right? Who will be playing drums?' 'I'll be playing drums.' 'Jon Lord?' 'Jon Lord will be playing organ'."

"It was going to be called The Light. And then he said: "And I will be playing bass and vocals!" So he was playing lead guitar, drums, bass and vocals! So, when I saw Jon, I said: 'What's going on? Is he a bit...' (making a circular motion by his temple with his index finger). So, after a while, we were playing together at this little house where Deep Purple started in Cadogan Gardens in South Kensington. But Chris was saying such ridiculous things. He was so ludicrous with what he wanted to do, and whoever the biggest band was at the time - I think it was Clapton and The Cream - they were going to be opening for us. He was nuts! The second time I went there the house looked like it had actually been hit by a bomb. There was rubble - no more furniture and carpets - just rubble! Someone had gone in with a pneumatic drill and drilled up everything. Plaster was down everywhere; then I saw some of the plaster move. It was Chris, who was sleeping on the floor. 'Ah, Ritchie, come on in. The band's great, it's all happening.' He was just full of bullshit, but a genuine rock 'n' roll character."

But Blackmore was impressed with Jon Lord who he saw performing with The Flowerpot Men at the California Ballroom, Dunstable on 8 December 1967. It was clearly a magical moment for both men that set the foundations for what followed. It was an event that Jon Lord remembered and relayed to the author forty years later. "When he first saw me play, I was actually in the backing band for the Flowerpot Men. But that backing band used to do solo spots and he came up to watch me play because he'd heard about how I played. Even in that band I was doing weird stuff with the draw bars on the organ and knocking the organ about and putting in bits of Bach and Tchaikovksy and God knows what in the solos, just to try and see... to push the boundaries for my own enjoyment and hopefully to be entertaining as well, because that is obviously what music is all about. It's not playing in a vacuum."

It was brought up when Blackmore visited Lord at the organist's flat in Fulham, and decided to try and get the band off the ground. "He and I had that conversation," Lord said. "And when we first got together he said, 'I came to see you play'. 'Oh really?' 'Yea at the California Ballroom in Dunstable' and he said, 'good stuff I like all that classical bit.' But then again he said 'I like it when you knock the organ about, I find that exciting' because he was just getting into that idea of what he had seen Hendrix do, thrashing the guitar about and see what he could make do of that."

Meanwhile Curtis was soon to drift out of the picture, but a press report published in the *New Musical Express* on 6 January 1968 throws a different light on the subject, albeit with some poetic licence. *Curtis has formed a new group of five multi-instrumentalists, which he will record individually and as a team. Named Roundabout, the group is rehearsing all this month, and at the end of January will cut its first LP, "Get On". Curtis is also planning a specially produced stage show complete with visual effects – the show will be a complete package, incorporating its own supporting acts and including another group formed by Curtis called Gates of Heaven. Personnel of the Roundabout comprises John Lord, Robbie Hewlett, Kenny Mudie, Ritchie Blackmore, Chris Curtis and another musician who cannot be named.*

Little information about Hewlett and Mudie is known, although a bassist called Robbie Hewlett played on a 1971 album called *The Lady*, by acoustic guitarist Allan Taylor and in 1981 was in a band called Choice, formed by Wishbone Ash guitarist David Alan "Ted" Turner. This is more than likely the same person. Even less information is available about Mudie, nor is it clear what his role was to be within the band. Curtis was both drummer and vocalist with The Searchers so it's unclear whether or not Mudie was to fulfil one of those roles or indeed a different one altogether. His name could also have been spelt incorrectly in the article (Lord's was) and could have been Moodie or Moody, but all variations have drawn a blank.

The talk of recording an album seems somewhat fanciful and the report in general gives some indication of Curtis's vivid imagination. His behaviour was certainly becoming more erratic in the eyes of Lord and Blackmore and before long Curtis drifted out of the equation.

With Lord and Blackmore at the helm, Blackmore then approached drummer Bobby Woodman: "I was in the London Speakeasy one night and I saw Ricky Blackmore and said 'hello'. He gave me the details of this band he was forming and asked me if I was interested in joining. I asked, 'what sort of band are you in?' Because I'm a rockabilly drummer. He said we're a rock 'n' roll band funded by millionaire businessmen."

Woodman recalls that along with Blackmore and Lord they started writing together but needed a singer. "I knew Dave Curtiss, a great bass player and singer. Dave was interested in joining, but Lord and Blackmore said he wasn't good looking enough. They didn't give him a chance."

Dave Curtiss had been lead vocalist with The Tremors, who'd had three singles released on the *Philips* label during 1963 and '64. But as Woodman points out he could also play bass. "I was in Paris working for Michel Pomareff at the time when Bobby rang me up and said this band was getting together and can I come over," recalls Curtiss. "So I did and met Jon Lord and Ritchie Blackmore sitting on a bed going through ideas for about a week or ten days. And nothing really occurred, so I said, 'I've got this gig in Paris,' and I just went. I hadn't met Blackmore or Lord before, but Bobby and I were a good unit, and I would've been a really good bass player for them, but Jon asked if I was as good as some big star like Jack Bruce, and I said I didn't compare myself to anyone, which was obviously not what he wanted to hear!"

With Curtiss returning to Paris, Lord brought in his colleague from the Flowerpot Men, bassist Nick Simper. All of this occurred over a matter of a few weeks, and by February Lord, Blackmore, Woodman and Simper had set up home at Deeves Hall, in South Mimms, Hertfordshire, where they started rehearsing and searching for a vocalist. "We were getting nowhere auditioning singers," says Simper. "We had put out feelers to Terry Reid and the reply came back through the management that he wasn't interested."

Reid has gone down in rock history for not only turning down what would become Deep Purple, but a few months later he also rejected Jimmy Page's invitation to join Led Zeppelin, and in doing so suggested Robert Plant in the process. It is generally considered that manager Mickie Most had such a tight control over Reid, that even if he wanted the job, Most was determined to retain him as a solo performer.

When speaking to *Classic Rock* magazine in 2006 Reid said: "I'm not sure what frame I was in when I was asked. I think it was when Ritchie was doing it at the beginning, or maybe afterwards, or maybe in between. I had gone to California and it's all a bit vague. But Blackmore was a brilliant guitar player. I saw him in Screaming Lord Sutch's Savages. Sutch used to chase him around the stage with an axe. Ritchie never used to miss a note and that ain't an easy thing to do. Not when you are about to be beheaded! Blackmore had a terrible job being a member of that band."

Nick Simper then suggested a vocalist from the same West London area that both he and Blackmore came from. Ian Gillan was someone that Simper had seen many years earlier when the young singer was performing under the name of Jess Thunder with his band The Javelins. By 1968 he had reverted to using his real name as lead singer with the pop outfit Episode Six. The group had recorded several singles, and had also appeared on the German TV show *Beat Beat Beat*.

When Gillan was approached for the newly created band he declined, believing that Episode Six, as an already established band was going to hit the big time, and had little reason to believe this new group would achieve much success. Simper: "I offered the job to Ian Gillan in the first place when we started, 'cause I knew him before these guys and he said. 'Oh, you're never gonna get anywhere, I'm gonna stay where I am, with Episode Six, 'cause we gonna make it big'."

Although some people dispute that Gillan was in the frame from the outset he confirmed that he was during an interview in France in 1976: "When they started they asked me to be their singer but I was happy in another group and I turned it down."

Ritchie Blackmore commented in 1971 that Mike Harrison was also on the short list. "He used to be in Spooky Tooth and had a girlfriend in Hamburg when I was there. He would be very big if he was better organised. We wanted to get him for Deep Purple when we started but he didn't want to know."

Another vocalist considered was the lead singer with the Jeff Beck Group - Rod Stewart. The guys went to check him out at London's Marquee club on 20 February. Blackmore was, and indeed still is to this day, a great admirer of Beck's guitar skills, but none of the band was suitably impressed with Stewart to even offer him an audition! It's probably worth mentioning that Stewart had also been one of the many vocalists to enter Joe Meek's studios several years earlier but the maverick producer was also unimpressed with the self-proclaimed 'Scottish' singer!

Another interesting fact concerning Stewart happened shortly after this. Simper recalled it was during Deep Purple's tour in Denmark, but it possibly occurred at the 8th National Jazz & Blues Festival at Sunbury-on-Thames on 8th August where both bands were on the bill. According to Simper, Blackmore was chatting to Stewart, and recalling the night at the Marquee earlier in the year, drew the singer in hook, line and sinker when he commented: "It was really great." Stewart apparently perked up, "yeah?" "Especially the bit when you went off stage for the band to do an instrumental" Blackmore quipped, leaving Beck's frontman somewhat deflated.

Resorting to placing adverts in *Melody Maker*, hordes of singers applied for the job, and Nick Simper had the task of collecting them from Borehamwood Railway station and ferrying the potentials to the remote farmhouse a few miles away. Amongst the many who applied was Mick Angus who sang with a Slough based band. Angus was so close to getting the job and confident that he had told his close friends in fellow Slough band The Maze, including singer Rod Evans. Evans then took the opportunity to apply for the gig himself. Evans impressed the majority of the band, not just with his vocal abilities but also with his song ideas, in particular his idea to do The Beatles 'Help!' as a ballad.

Having made a rod for their own back by disregarding one Scottish singer, by March, and to the surprise of Angus, they had finally found their vocalist with Edinburgh-born Evans. Woodman, however wasn't so impressed by The Maze's front man: "Rod Evans got up and sung some Frank Sinatra numbers and I thought, 'we don't want this kind of singer'."

Although Evans appointment completed the five-man outfit the rest of the band was becoming increasingly disillusioned with Woodman. Blackmore, Lord and Simper were drawn to the sounds of Hendrix, and in particular the American East Coast band Vanilla Fudge, with its leanings towards psychedelia and lengthy instrumental jams. Woodman, who had worked with traditional rock 'n' roll stars like Vince Taylor and Johnny Hallyday was at odds with the musical direction the band was heading in.

Many years later Woodman openly admitted that he wasn't happy with the way things were developing: "They played this song and I said, "You sound like a fucking circus band! Can we play something that's to do with the band and stop wasting time?"

As Lord recalled, "Rod pulled me to one side and said, "Our drummer Ian is a much better drummer than Bobby"." In 1972 Paice recalled the series of events from his perspective: "Rod said he had an audition with this new band and he was leaving." The Maze was earning good money for the time, going out for £5 a night, and they weren't keen to jack it in. "Rod took me to one side and said, "Look they've got a drummer at the moment but I think they'll like you better." So I went along and found out that it was Blackmore."

Paice also recalled meeting Blackmore the previous year at the Star Club, Hamburg. "This is where I ran into Ritchie. He'd been there a year, sort of stagnating. He sent his girlfriend up to me and she said Ritchie would like to offer me a job. I went 'Oh really!' 'Cos I'd heard of him. I thought great. So I said what's he got and she said he didn't have a band yet. So I said I was sorry and I went back home."

Blackmore also remembered seeing The Maze in Hamburg the previous year. Woodman was replaced and Deep Purple was born, although they were still working on Curtis's name of Roundabout, largely on the insistence of manager Tony Edwards.

Tony Edwards, along with his fellow investors John Coletta and Ron Hire under the management name of HEC Enterprises were financing the operation from the outset although the band didn't formally sign a management deal with HEC until 3rd September. Ian Paice's father Keith was also a signatory on account of Paice still being under 21.

By this time the debut album *Shades of Deep Purple* had been released and as a gesture it was dedicated to Bobby Woodman, Chris Curtis and Dave Curtiss, who had clearly played a part in the band's formation.

The first song

The opening track on *Shades of Deep Purple* was fittingly the instrumental Blackmore / Lord composition 'And The Address'. This was the very first song that Blackmore and Lord worked on together when they convened at Jon Lord's London flat in December 1967. As Lord recalled many years later: "Ritchie came to the flat. He appeared at my door in a snowstorm, carrying an acoustic guitar. That night we came up with two of the songs that went on the first album, 'And The Address' and 'Mandrake Root'. It was a wonderful evening. Right away I felt that he wouldn't suffer fools gladly, but it felt right. Ritchie seemed dark, he always seemed dark."

Although they came up with the riff, the title came later. To most people it would seem to be extremely innocent, but the phrase was used frequently in musician circles in the sixties, and would appear to have derived from the time bands spent squeezed together in small vans as they toured the country. When one of them encountered flatulence, the common response was, "and the address..."

As for the other song, 'Mandrake Root', it wasn't entirely original and not for the last time Purple would lift a riff from elsewhere. Although the title was used by Blackmore for a short lived band he had in Germany earlier that year, "Mandrake Root was written by a guy called Bill Parkinson and it was called 'Lost Soul' originally," explains Nick Simper. "He was with Sutch before Ritchie (re-joined) and they used to do that as one of the opening numbers. When Ritchie took over, Carlo (Little, drummer) taught him the melody note for note, sung it to him. Ritchie said, 'what about this?' I said, 'that's Bill's number 'Lost Soul',' 'Not now it isn't.' I said 'you won't get away with that' but the attitude was 'just watch me'."

Dave Dee, Ritchie, Jon, Nick and Titch

Deep Purple's first show took place on 20 April 1968 at the Park School in Vestpoppen, Taastrup, Denmark. The decision to gig first in the Scandinavian country was due to the popularity Jon Lord had achieved there with his previous band The Artwoods, who also toured Denmark after cashing in on the gangster fad and renaming itself St. Valentine's Day Massacre. From the outset there was a notable amount of press interest, and several reviews of the gig were printed in the Danish media.

En krydsning af de engelske Artwoods og Flover Potmen er blevet til Roundabout, og dette orkester

Even though the band had decided to scrap the name Roundabout on the ferry journey there, it still wasn't clear to all, and many reviewers referred to them as Roundabout. Lord and John Coletta were interviewed during the tour and Lord commented about the Roundabout name. "I've driven around so many roundabouts in my time without even thinking that the name might have been patented. But there was no way around it. We had to change our name to avoid an awful lot of trouble. But in any case the new name seems okay."

Some reviewers focused on the amount of gear and the volume generated. One report simply stated, *the sheer amount of complicated equipment put up and readied prior to Roundabout's debut reminded me of the preparations for a Cape Kennedy rocket launch. The soundwave that penetrated the stage curtain as the band took to the stage only helped to*

22

confirm my associations with rockets. *An infernal noise ripping your ears into bloody pieces.* As Lord told the Danish press, "I know we're loud onstage, but you need to be to reach the youth of today. We're not loud just for the sake of being loud, you just have to make sure people don't think they're at a tea party, because then they'll lose interest."

Whilst the reviews were generally favourable, Carsten Grolin's initial thoughts after the first three songs and the band's appearance prompted the comment, *Roundabout, with make-up on their faces, dyed and teased hair, and far too shiny clothes, fumbled around on the worst side of sexy pop music, and resembled nothing so much as an unfunny parody of Dave Dee, Dozy, Beaky, Mick and Titch. We shivered in the cold room and began to look for a corner to hide in. There's nothing quite as embarrassing as watching good friends die on stage.*

Fortunately though Grolin saw something else in the band as well. *All of a sudden Roundabout shook off the excesses and decided they weren't going to be Dave Dee after all, but rather wanted instead to be themselves. They suddenly seemed different as they grew along with the music. It began to take shape during the Vanilla Fudge and Nice inspired 'Mandrake Root', with its sharply punctuated and elegant rhythmic surprises amidst improvisations from each instrument.*

Grolin also paid compliments to the "sexy vocalist" Rod Evans in his shiny clothes for his soulful vocal performance on 'Help!' He concluded his

A rare photo from the first gig.

review by saying, *when Roundabout get their rich collective talents together and forget about Dave Dee, they will become a force to be reckoned with.*

Despite the promising start, success in Europe was by and large, still some considerable way off whilst instant success in America occurred with the debut single 'Hush'. However 'Hush' was also a big hit in one European country – Switzerland. Four months on from the debut gig and Purple travelled to Berne in Switzerland on a multi-band bill that included the Small Faces in a 4,000 seat venue. Unfortunately the police had to move in with batons to quell trouble as the show ended in chaos after the fans swarmed the stage after just two numbers by one of the bands. The group in question? Well it was none other than Dave Dee, Dozy, Beaky, Mick and Titch! I wonder which band had the shiniest shirts that night?

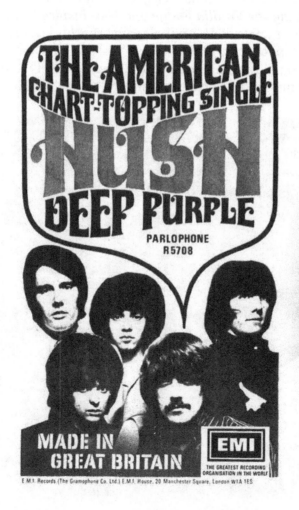

Blackmore's Country & Western playing prevents a beating!

The exact destination and date is long forgotten but during one of Purple's first American tours, following a gig in what Nick Simper described as "red-neck territory", both he and Blackmore decided to check out the local bars. Much of America at the time took a dim view to men with long hair and the band had encountered hostility and dismissive comments almost from the moment they stepped on US soil. Rod Evans nearly got in a fight when locals "wolf-whistled" the band as they walked down a New York street, but his fellow band members convinced him it wasn't a wise move.

On the occasion of Blackmore's near mishap he and Simper walked in to a club where country musicians were performing. Blackmore had always had an interest in country music and was a great admirer of Albert Lee, one of England's finest country pickers.

As soon as the pair were inside they felt the beady eyes of the local rednecks upon them and a distinctly uncomfortable air pervaded. After what seemed like an eternity and following hostile comments, Blackmore thought on his feet, knowing that the only way not to lose face or end up having to run for their lives, would be to let his guitar playing do the talking. He stepped up on the stage and started playing with the resident band.

During his days as a session player for producer Joe Meek, Blackmore had been required to play country style on numerous occasions and even toured around Ireland for three weeks with country singer Houston Wells. With consummate ease his playing soon won over the hostile rednecks and before long the Deep Purple musicians were welcomed into the fray and gifted beers. A potentially ugly scene had been averted.

Fifteenth Century masterpiece costs Purple dearly

There is no doubt that America is a land of great contradictions. Despite its reputation as the land of the free, the powers that be have always had an issue with nudity. Deep Purple's self-titled third album was released in the States in June 1969, but soon became the centre of a controversy. The cover used a section of the right hand panel of the *Garden of Earthly Delights* triptych by renowned master painter Hieronymous Bosch (c. 1450 – 9 August 1516) but some took offence at its nude figures. It was painted in either the late fifteenth or early sixteenth century and is considered to be Bosch's most accomplished work. The imagery depicts his vision of Hell, with the nude figures having lost all their eroticism. During the Middle Ages, sexuality and lust were seen, by some, as evidence of man's fall from grace, and the most foul of the seven deadly sins. Because of its content it had been displayed at the Vatican, but as far as the Americans were concerned, the work was wrongly perceived as containing profane images, despite the original being marvelled by thousands every year at the Prado in Madrid. As such many US stores refused to display it.

Whilst the original was painted in full colour, the monochrome

NOW DEEP PURPLE ARE HIT BY ALBUM COVER BAN

BLIND FAITH hit the MM headlines last week when their album cover — showing an 11-year-old nude girl — was banned in the States.

Now Deep Purple have run into trouble with the cover of their latest album — which has been banned from open displays in America.

Reason: It includes some nude figures in a black-and-white reproduction of "The Garden Of Earthly Delights," a triptych by 14-century artist Heironymus Bosch, which hung in the Vatican for many years and is now on display in Prado, Madrid.

Comments Anthony Edwards, of HEC, Deep Purple's management: "It does seem particularly weird that in one or two of the more puritanical States they are taking exception to a painting which has been displayed for so long in one of the great religious

centres of the world."

Meanwhile, Deep Purple and the Royal Philharmonic Orchestra conducted by Malcolm Arnold are to appear in a concert together at London's Royal Albert Hall on Wednesday, September 24.

Jon Lord, Deep Purple organist, is writing a special orchestral work for the occasion, which will combine the five members of the group and the Royal Philharmonic Orchestra on the concert platform.

Just issued is Deep Purple's new single, "Hallelujah."

reproduction on the Purple album was evidently a mistake. It also had the addition of a band photograph; designed to blend in, rather crudely pasted on. But colour or not, with many American stores refusing to put it on display, sales were undoubtedly hindered.

Purple manager Tony Edwards conveyed his disappointment and bemusement with the attitude of some. "It does seem particularly weird that in one or two of the more Puritanical States they are taking exception to a painting which has been displayed for so long in one of the great religious centres of the world."

What makes the situation even more ridiculous is that an American band One Nation Underground had used the same art on the cover of its debut album *Pearls Before Swine* released two years earlier.

With the band's US label *Tetragrammaton* already starting to suffer financially, Purple's popularity had already taken a dip since the hit single 'Hush' the previous year, but the treatment metered out by some US retailers didn't exactly help matters. Maybe they should have done what the record company in Australia opted for and released the album in a plain purple sleeve.

By early 1970 *Tetragrammaton* ceased trading and the American Puritans got their way, as the album disappeared altogether. The same applied to Canada. Even though Purple's records there were released on *Polydor*, they were *Tetragrammaton* productions. *Polydor* Canada did manage to release a couple of compilations from the first three albums in 1970 with *The Best of Deep Purple* and *Early Purple* in 1972. Even when *Warner Bros* took on Purple the following year and took ownership of the

DEEP PURPLE

Produced by Derek Lawrence

SIDE 1   T - 119

1. CHASING SHADOWS (Lord-Paice) 5:32
2. BLIND (Lord) 5:21
3. LALEÑA (Donovan) 5:02
4. FAULTLINE 5:34
   (Lord-Blackmore-Paice-Simper)
THE PAINTER
   (Lord-Blackmore-Evans-Paice-Simper)

STEREO

Tetragrammaton back catalogue, they did not re-release the album, and along with the other two MKI LPs they remained unavailable in America for decades. *Warners* did release a compilation of the three albums in 1972 called *Purple Passages*. It included a previously unissued mix of 'The Bird Has Flown'. With the third album particularly difficult to find, half of the album's eight tracks were included on the compilation but needless to say there was no sign of Bosch's imagery included!

Rod Evans sits down on the job

The third album *Deep Purple* saw the band continue its development towards the heavier sound, which has become Purple's trademark. It also showed the writing skills from within the band coming to the fore. As a consequence there was only one cover tune, 'Lalena' by Donovan. It was also the only out and out ballad on the album and was arguably Rod Evans' finest vocal performance.

Also, despite the general heavier sound for the majority of their stage act, 'Lalena' was a popular part of the live set. Evans had developed a stage persona that included much gyrating around and prompted the sort of comments of comparison with Dave Dee, Dozy, Beaky, Mick and Titch as outlined from that review of the first gig. But for 'Lalena', as had also been the case for 'Help!' from the very first gigs, Evans adopted an entirely different approach as he sat at the front of the stage to deliver his heartfelt rendition of Donovan's lament to a woman driven to prostitution.

When Nick Simper started touring the *Deep Purple MKI Songbook* in 2010 with Austrian band Nasty Habits he relayed to vocalist Christian Schmidt of Evans' cross-legged singing and the young Austrian did likewise during the gigs that saw Simper and the band bring the early Purple songs back to life.

Live at The Marquee or all at sea?

Since the early sixties the legendary status of London's Marquee Club should not be underestimated within the British rock music scene. Some consider the Marquee the most important venue in European popular music history and just about every major British act has played at the legendary London club. As with many of London's venues it started as a Jazz club, originally located at 165 Oxford Street, where it opened its doors for the first time on 19 April 1958. The Marquee soon became an important place for Jazz as well as the Rhythm & Blues scene, and The Rolling Stones apparently played their first ever gig there in July 1962. It was when the club moved to Wardour Street on 13 March 1964 that the Marquee soon developed the truly legendary reputation it now holds. Through the decade that followed, it witnessed some of the biggest names in the early part of their careers: Jimi Hendrix, David Bowie, Cream, Pink Floyd, Elton John, The Who, The Nice, Yes, Jethro Tull, King Crimson, Genesis, Moody Blues and many others. Bands such as The Yardbirds and The Animals were regulars and it was also the venue that launched the first ever gig by Led Zeppelin, under the name of the New Yardbirds.

Before 1970 The Marquee didn't have a drinks licence so it was a common practice for people to nip into The Ship pub across the street both before the shows and during the intermissions. This wasn't just the case for the audience but for the bands as well. The Ship was definitely the place to rub shoulders with the rock fraternity during the glory years of the sixties and seventies, and Ritchie Blackmore was one of many who spent time at the venue during the mid sixties.

In fact he played there as part of Lord Sutch's band in May '65. The following year Jon Lord appeared at the Marquee on no less than four occasions with his then band The Artwoods. For The Artwoods second appearance on 3rd October, they were supported by MI5, the Slough based band featuring Ian Paice and Rod Evans. MI5 made a second appearance on the 14th November as support to The Alan Bown Set. That same year Episode Six, featuring Ian Gillan and Roger Glover made six support slot appearances including one to Cliff Bennett & the Rebel Rousers (one of Gillan's favourite singers), and another to the Spencer Davis Group.

When Deep Purple formed in 1968 they played some of their earliest shows in small clubs around the UK, but spent much of the first eighteen months in America. After the collapse of the band's US record label in late 1969, they focused their attention back in Britain.

Given the array of British acts that did play the Marquee, it would be natural to assume that Purple was amongst them. In fact an advert appeared in *Melody Maker* for a Deep Purple concert at the Marquee for Tuesday 9

September 1969; fifteen days before the performance of Jon Lord's *Concerto For Group & Orchestra* at the Royal Albert Hall. However it never actually took place. The band was touring Scandinavia until the 7th, but some of the band missed the ferry crossing back, so it had to be cancelled.

The nearest that Deep Purple got to playing the Marquee Club was when they played in the marquee the previous year! Confused? Read on... On 10 August 1968 the band appeared at The Eighth National Jazz and Blues Festival at Kempton Park Racecourse, Sunbury-on-Thames. The Marquee Club was jointly involved with presenting the festival, and aside from the main stage there was a marquee stage erected on site. Within the festival program the Marquee Club delighted in stating, *Artists appearing at this festival can be seen at our West End showcase... the famous Marquee Club.* But Deep Purple had only played a handful of gigs in England before this appearance, and none of them were at The Marquee Club.

As it was, Deep Purple was one of only two acts (Joe Cocker was the other) on that day to play both the main stage and the marquee. They were the first band on the main stage at 7:00pm, playing a half hour set, and followed this with a 45 minute set at 9:00 pm inside the marquee.

By 1974, by which time Deep Purple's popularity was immense, and they were playing to huge audiences in America and elsewhere, when tour plans for the MKIII line-up's UK debut were announced in the music press at the beginning of the year, a spokesman for the band claimed that the intentions were to get back to playing smaller places and the Marquee was mentioned as one of the venues under consideration. Alas when the tour was finalised, Deep Purple played three gigs

in the capital at Hammersmith Odeon, Lewisham Odeon, and the Kilburn State Gaumont. All the venues were considerably smaller than Wembley Empire Pool or Earls Court, but clearly the Marquee was considered too small for a band of Purple's then stature.

So despite playing other London clubs such as The Speakeasy in '68 and '69, it can be categorically stated that Deep Purple was one of very few of the heavyweight acts never to have played the Marquee, although individual band

members did so throughout the seventies and beyond. Nick Simper's band Warhorse played the Marquee twice in 1971. Trapeze were regulars in 1973, appearing four times in January and February with Blackmore, Lord and Paice amongst the audiences before inviting the band's vocalist / bassist, Glenn Hughes to join Purple that summer.

Ian Gillan played at The Marquee several times with various incarnations of his own band during the seventies, including one occasion on Wednesday 27 December 1978 with Ritchie Blackmore joining in for the encore. Blackmore showed up again on Monday 18 August 1989, getting up on stage to jam with Girl for one song.

At Deep Purple's show at Wembley Arena on 3 March 1987, Gillan remarked to the audience "welcome to the Marquee." This concert was released as a bootleg called *The Antiques Roadshow* and some non-UK fans were taken in by his off the cuff quip, believing it to be a secret performance during the arena tour. Alas it was not so.

Despite that, Purple never got to perform there. Ian Gillan's lyrics on the nostalgic based song '69', from the band's 1998 album *Abandon* reference the venue and its manager Jack Barrie: *Ligging at the Old Marquee, spinning Jack a line, even he knew better than me, back in sixty nine.*

Government in Bradford

Having changed the line-up in June '69 with Ian Gillan and Roger Glover replacing Evans and Simper the new members fitted in perfectly and there was an instant chemistry. However the financial problems encountered by the US record company temporarily prevented further gigging in the States. It gave them no option other than to focus on gigging as much as possible within their homeland. It was quite a change as the venues around the country were smaller and earned them less money than they had been commanding across the Atlantic. Even after the performance of Jon Lord's *Concerto For Group & Orchestra* at the Royal Albert Hall in September, they continued to take whatever gigs they could. On 22 November they played at Bradford University, supported by a semi-pro band from the North East by the name of the Government. Their lead singer was David Coverdale: "I remember playing on the bill with them a few years before just after the second chapter of the band. I remember being complimented a lot by Ritchie, Jon and Roger."

Malcolm Buckton, bassist with The Government recalled, "After they had finished their sound check and lifted the roof we had our chance and warmed up with our version of 'Shakin' All Over' which was met with generous applause from Jon Lord and Ian Paice."

It's often been said that Jon Lord took Coverdale's number in case the new vocalist didn't work out, but the fact was, Ian Gillan was already working out. It was more a case of the eighteen-year-old Coverdale volunteering his services. Coverdale was aware that Gillan had only replaced Evans a few months earlier and having been complimented by the band, chanced his arm by giving Lord his phone number, more in the hope that having changed singers once, they might do the same again.

Coverdale hung on to the dream for a few weeks, hoping to get a call but a few weeks turned in to a few years before he eventually got his opportunity, by which time he had to promote himself again. Nearly four years had elapsed from that gig in Bradford, but eventually David Coverdale did get his just rewards and became Deep Purple's third singer in August '73.

Money for reviewing, get your gigs for free!

Barely two weeks after the gig in Bradford where David Coverdale's band supported, Purple were back in the West Yorkshire city, this time at the larger St Georges Hall. Another musician who was to find success years later was in the hall that night but in a different working capacity.

Mark Knopfler who found fame and fortune with Dire Straits started his working life as a journalist. He left home to attend journalism school at the age of 17. In 1968, after studying journalism for a year at Harlow Technical College, Knopfler graduated and landed a job as a reporter and music critic at the *Yorkshire Evening Post*, where he stayed for two years.

Elsewhere, despite Deep Purple's profile having risen, following the performance of Jon Lord's *Concerto For Group & Orchestra* at the Royal Albert Hall, three months earlier, they were still in the process of trying to establish themselves within the UK.

On 7 December 1969 Purple supported Family at St George's Hall, Bradford. Knopfler was sent along to review the gig: *Great show from Purple and Family. The Family and Purple concert at St. George's Hall, Bradford on Sunday, really did come up to expectations. DP belted out their usual stupefying act with Ritchie Blackmore's roasting solos and Jon Lord's magnificent organ work. The group ended with 'Mandrake Root', complete with strobe light, feedback and general disrespect shown to amplification equipment and musical instruments. Quite astonishing nevertheless.*

As an aside, playing two shows in Bradford a fortnight apart may well have had an effect on Ian Gillan. On 21st December he wrote a poem entitled *Lucifer in Bradford*. It was later published in *Candy Horizon* (see page 58).

Deep Purple of course broke through in the UK the following year with the release of *In Rock* and 'Black Night'. For Knopfler, after two years with the *Yorkshire Evening Post*, he pursued an English degree at Leeds University, where he graduated in 1973.

Knopfler then moved to London to pursue his career in music. A struggling musician, he moved into a room that had no heat and slept on an ambulance stretcher instead of a bed. Finally, he decided to get a job teaching English part-time at Loughton College for a more stable income, and he worked there until 1977 when he formed Dire Straits along with his brother David on rhythm guitar, Pick Withers on drums and bass player John Illsley.

Ironically shortly before Dire Straits was formed, Purple's eight years of success had come to an end. Dire Straits met with huge success during the next few years, but coincidentally had their greatest success in 1985 with the release of *Brothers In Arms*. By then Deep Purple had reformed and the same year was also hugely successful with their first reunion tour being the second biggest grossing in America that year after Bruce Springsteen.

Deep Purple... Nice

Whilst it's fashionable to comment on rivalry between bands during the late sixties / early seventies period when Deep Purple was establishing itself, in general there was nothing but camaraderie. A point in case being Deep Purple's friendship with The Nice, and in particular keyboard player Keith Emerson. Having started as the backing band for American soul singer P.P Arnold, The Nice set off on a different path in mid-67, forging rock with classical ideas.

In February '69 Purple shared a bill with The Nice at London's University College. Jon Lord and Emerson became good friends throughout this period. Towards the end of the year both keyboard men also premiered their first works combining the band with an orchestra. Lord's *Concerto For Group & Orchestra* was premiered on 24th September at the Royal Albert Hall, and Emerson's *Five Bridges Suite* just 16 days later at the Newcastle Arts Festival. A second recorded performance followed a week later at the less salubrious Fairfield Halls. Something that Emerson jokingly remarked about after Lord's death in 2012: "In the early years I remember being quite jealous of Jon Lord – may he rest in peace. In September 1969 I heard he was debuting his *Concerto For Group & Orchestra* at the Royal Albert Hall, with none other than Malcolm Arnold conducting. Wow! I had to go along and see that. Jon and I ribbed each other, we were pretty much pals, but I walked away and thought: 'Shit, in a couple of weeks time I'm going to be recording The

Nice's *Five Bridges Suite*... not at the Albert Hall but at the Fairfield Halls, Croydon!' A much more prosaic venue."

It's probably worth pointing out however that The Nice had been banned from playing the Royal Albert Hall following a performance there on 26 June 1968 when Emerson burned an American flag onstage during a performance of 'America' at a *Come Back Africa* charity event.

Deep Purple and The Nice shared the same stage again on 30 March 1970. This time it was in Berlin, at the *Peace Pop World Festival*, which was supposedly The Nice's last concert, although a poster for the *Progressive Pop Festival* in Cologne on April 4 lists them, along with Deep Purple as amongst the acts performing. But back to Berlin and Deep Purple took the stage first, performing a typically usual set for the time, opening with three numbers from the as then, unreleased *In Rock* album; 'Speed King', 'Child in Time' and 'Into the Fire'. The set continued with two instrumentals from the previous line-up, 'Wring That Neck' and Purple's version of 'Paint It, Black' and the main set finished with 'Mandrake Root'. For the encore they returned with Keith Emerson joining them for rousing versions of Roy Orbison's 'Go! Go! Go! (Down the Line)' and Little Richard's 'Lucille'.

The Nice performed their usual combination of rock and classical compositions such as 'Intermezzo From Karelia Suite', 'Hang On To A Dream' and 'Country Pie/Brandenburg Concerto No. 6'. For their encore Ritchie Blackmore and Ian Gillan joined them for a lengthy jam - a nice way to conclude the band's career. Soon after Keith Emerson teamed up with Greg Lake and Carl Palmer for one of the first supergroups, ELP.

Several months later Deep Purple had its second foray into rock music with an orchestra, when Lord's *Gemini Suite* was performed at London's Royal Festival Hall. Lord spoke to *Disc and Music Echo* about the band's future and recent past. "The *Gemini Suite* we were asked to do. It's not everyday you get asked by the *BBC* to do something like that. But as a group we have decided not to do anymore for the time being although we might feel like it in a year's time. I don't know - it's not Ritchie's scene."

But Lord clearly still had ambitions within that sphere: "I have written things for orchestra that I'd like to get performed, that's my eventual aim. I'd like to write an organ concerto for Keith Emerson. We did talk about it about six months ago but we didn't have time. We did think about doing a double album - The Nice with an orchestra on one, and us with another orchestra on the other. But the financial problems would have been ridiculous. But I'd certainly like to write something for him - his technique seems to have no limits but it would be just him and an orchestra, no group."

Lord had also been asked by the *BBC* to write another composition, and was given until June '71 to complete it. "I don't know what I want to do. I want to talk to Keith about it. I'd love to play piano with an orchestra. Perhaps it could be Keith on organ, me on piano and an orchestra. There will be about four or five movements and we could swap over in the middle. It would be great to write."

With Purple's ever-growing touring and recording schedule any such plans to compose a piece involving Keith Emerson never materialised. Jon did however find time to re-write and record a studio version of *Gemini Suite* in March '71. Again, following Lord's death Emerson recalled that, "Jon wanted me to play on his solo album, *Gemini Suite*, but that was around the time Emerson Lake & Palmer were breaking big and we were touring. He was a lovely guy, a real gentleman."

By 1974 both Lord with Purple, and Emerson with ELP were amongst the biggest selling bands in the world and their paths crossed once again at the California Jam but this time there was no chance of any of the Purple guys joining Emerson and Co. on stage. Although Purple were officially the headliners they agreed to ELP closing the all-day event, as it gave them more time to move on to the next gig the following day in Phoenix, Arizona. As anyone who has seen the video of the concert will know, Blackmore's antics towards an *ABC* television camera necessitated a hasty exit anyway!

Emerson's connection with Purple continued when he contributed to a charity recording of 'Smoke On The Water' in 1989 (see page 176) and it emerged again in 1998 when the reformed ELP supported Purple on its US tour. The same year, Glenn Hughes performed at three concerts by Marc Bonilla and Friends, which also included Emerson. An album *Boys Club Live From California* was released several years later. In 1999 Emerson appeared on Hughes' solo album *The Way it Is* and Hughes recorded vocals for a version of ELP's 'Knife Edge' for a tribute album entitled *Encores, Legends & Paradox*.

Somebody Stole My Guitar

On 28 February 1970 at the Philharmonic Hall in Liverpool Ritchie Blackmore was the victim of theft from right under his nose when his prized black *Fender Stratocaster* was stolen as a result of a rather comical incident involving his roadie Ian Hansford.

During the climactic ending to 'Mandrake Root' the excitement was enhanced by strobe lighting. Although adding effect for the audience it potentially brought problems on stage as Hansford explains, "In 'Mandrake Root' when it went into the strobe lights occasionally he had an old guitar, which he would smash hell out of and if we could use it again I'd bolt it back together but this night he's at the front of the stage, he's rubbing up and down the stage with it. It's in his hand, not round his neck- he's got the strap off and the lead came out- the jack plug. He comes running back to me and I run back to him and with these strobe lights... you know how deceiving they are - the eyes and the mind play tricks on you and we crashed head on. We were both seeing stars and god knows what. We both had splitting headaches. By the time he'd picked up his other guitar and I'd gone to the front of the stage it had gone. People at the front of the stage must have thought it was part of the act. We had to go out looking round the streets for twenty minutes after that. I was not in favour - it was all my fault. Then we had a couple of days off before we went to Switzerland... In the meantime this kid came home with a *Fender Stratocaster* and one of his parents said where did you get this from and got in touch with the hall. Roger Brewer who used to help us out on a gig basis went up on the train and brought the guitar back with him and Ritchie was a happy boy when I saw him in Switzerland and apologies all round."

Later in the year they returned to Liverpool in September but they were involved in a motorway accident on the way to the gig. Although no one was injured

£100 REWARD

for recovery or return (no questions asked) of GUITAR stolen from

DEEP PURPLE

by over-enthusiastic admirer(s)

last Saturday, February 28th

from stage of

Philharmonic Hall

LIVERPOOL

Description: Black Fender Stratocaster, with white scratch plate, maple neck and extra large tremolo arm. Serial number: 221737

Write or phone:

HEC ENTERPRISES
25 NEWMAN STREET
LONDON, W.1
Tel. 01-636 3911

they didn't get to the venue, St George's Hall, until 10.30pm. It was too late to do the gig so it was rescheduled for November.

Although Blackmore had his beloved black Strat back it didn't last for too long as he explained to *Guitar* magazine three years later. "After I got it back I went to Boston and smashed it up! I suddenly realised what I'd done - threw it into the audience - it was such a great audience. Came on stage again: 'God that was my black one. What can I do? Get it back?' It was in pieces by then; gone."

Strangely a similar incident occurred in 1995 at London's Hammersmith Apollo. Blackmore had left Purple by then and reformed Rainbow and towards the end of a blistering show left the guitar at the front of the stage. Before he knew it, someone had grabbed it and made a dash for the exit. Fortunately on this occasion Ritchie's roadie Rob Fodder rushed out of the stage door and around to the front of the building. The culprit was apprehended before he got out of the venue and was persuaded to take the guitar back to the stage. It was a highly surreal sight as he walked down the aisle with Blackmore's *Stratocaster* above his head, but even more bizarre was the fact that he was rewarded with an after show pass for returning the guitar!

Future British Prime Minister bunked off school to watch Deep Purple

On 20 March 1970 Deep Purple was at the Edinburgh Odeon for the start of a six-date Scottish tour. Amongst the audience that night were several lads from the local independent school Fettes: a traditional British public boarding school and a bastion that remained locked in traditional values where indiscipline was met with swift and harsh punishment.

In such schools, boarders were restricted in their movements and were not free to leave as they pleased. With the Purple concert falling on a Friday evening several of the pupils wanted to attend but the house rules confined them to the school. However a group of the senior boys were determined to see Deep Purple perform live.

One of those boys told his story to the *Mail On Sunday* in 2005. Despite the event taking place thirty-five years earlier, he still requested that he remained unidentified: "Four of us decided to break out of the school - in civvies of course - and go along. This was no simple undertaking. We were breaking the school rules in a serious way and knew that the consequences of being caught could be expulsion. We had to slip out of our respective houses and scale the school's twelve-foot perimeter wall without being seen. It was great fun, shinning down drainpipes. We managed all this and went straight to the Odeon mighty proud of ourselves. When we got inside the foyer we soon realised that we weren't the only boys from Fettes - there were another ten

How Deep Purple proved that our slippery PM never carries the can

IT WAS a long time ago, a few days before the Easter holidays in a year that had already seen Britain plunged into economic crisis.

Certainly that weekend it was not cool to be confined to school. Not if you were stuck in Edinburgh where the hugely popular psychedelic rock band Deep Purple were featuring at the local Odeon.

But while the year marked the zenith of hippydom and liberal culture, the world of Fettes, a bastion of privileged education north of the border, remained locked in traditional values where indiscipline was met with swift and harsh punishment.

This, however, did not stop a group of the school's senior boys who were determined to see Deep Purple perform live. Among them was Anthony Lynton Blair, a 17-year-old with a passion for rock that, if we are to believe him, lasts to this day

who had done exactly the same thing - among them 17-year-old Tony Blair, a lad with a passion for rock that lasts to this day."

was the one who snitched but I know for a fact that he wasn't. Instead, he had done something, made some kind of deal, who knows, to get out of being punished. We never found out what it was

us a lot about the man and just how far back he began honing his ability to skirt blame.

And while the Prime Minister's contemporary at Fettes assures me that Blair did not grass on his chums to spare his own skin, one has to wonder what else could have saved him from a caning.

Perhaps a hastily prepared

"We watched the concert and Deep Purple were fabulous. By the time we got back to school it was about 3am. We got back in okay and thought, wrongly as it turned out, that we had got away with it. But our misdemeanour was announced at breakfast and all 14 of us - Blair included - were told to report to the headmaster's office at 10:30. Only 13 turned up - Blair went missing. You might think that he was the one who snitched but I know for a fact that he wasn't. Instead, he had done something, made some kind of deal, who knows, to get out of being punished. We never found out what it was."

"We were all given the option of expulsion or the 'headmaster's punishment' which, I seem to remember, was six of the best. We all opted for the cane. It was all pretty trivial looking back. But I think it says quite a lot about Tony Blair and the way that, even as a 17-year-old, he was able to slither out of trouble."

Blair's passion for rock has not waned. Before he became the United Kingdom's Prime Minister and was still leader of the opposition he wrote to Ritchie Blackmore telling him of his admiration for his guitar playing. This should come as no surprise and clearly seeing Purple as a 17-year-old left a lasting impression.

A year after becoming Prime Minister, at the Conservative party conference, the then Shadow Culture Minister Peter Ainsworth launched a blistering attack on Blair. He called the Prime Minister a "frustrated rock star", and went on to condemn his "flashy parties at Number 10 with pop stars" as the "cringe" of a "middle-aged politician going through a phase of self-conscious trendiness."

Blair must only have fuelled Ainsworth's ire when he nominated the *Fender Stratocaster* guitar as the "symbol of the century". It might not have impressed his political rivals but Blackmore and Deep Purple fans alike may well share those sentiments.

Blackmore plays gig in the dressing room!

On 12 June 1970, having just returned from a three-gig stint in Germany, Purple played at the famous Eel Pie Island Club in Twickenham, South London, situated in the middle of the River Thames. Although it was best suited to blues bands with less equipment than Deep Purple used, it was still a worthwhile gig, despite the added difficulties in getting the gear to the venue via the only route, a narrow bridge. "You couldn't get the van across there. They used to have two Morris Minor Travellers we had to put everything in them and there was only two inches either side of the bridge to drive over. We had to park one side of the bridge and ferry everything over, then the same thing after the gig," remembers roadie Ian Hansford.

But that was just the start of the difficulties. Quite often Blackmore would get in a strop during soundchecks if things weren't to his liking, but without fully grasping the situation as Hansford explains. "If he didn't like the sound at the rehearsal he'd really get the hump. You couldn't get it over to him that it would be different when there are people in there. It might not be a totally good sound but at least people would soak it up. It would be echoing and bouncing all over the place but he'd really get the hump."

But at the Eel Pie Club on this particular evening other factors were also affecting Blackmore's decision making. Allied to a tiny stage area, there was water in the building. "When we got there it was flooded, the floor was awash, The Thames must have been really high, and he played the set in the changing room," says Hansford. "He said to me 'go and put a bit more top on the amp.' I can remember Jon Lord was furious, 'get him out here.' 'It's no good Jon, if I asked him to get out here is he going to say yes?' He might have started on stage but then he disappeared. I would say it was at least for three quarters of the set."

It was an incident that Jon Lord remembered very well when the author interviewed him in 2008: "It was funny because I knew Eel Pie really well because I'd played there with the Artwoods: We'd had a weekly residency for nearly two years I think, so I knew the club well and I knew it was a skanky old place and damp and odd, and the stage was cramped. It was quite early on and he was still learning how to control that *Stratocaster* and the amplification he wanted, the sound he had in his head. He was out there on the stage for the first ten or fifteen minutes; couldn't control the amp; he was too close to it. So he did what was in his mind a very logical thing to do. He went and sat away from the amplifier, and the only place he could find was the dressing room! Which was right behind the stage, so he played from there. It was typical Blackmore. As you say, there was an element of curmudgeonous in it but there was also an element of logic in it: Certainly logic as he saw it. He certainly does have a very special kind of logic."

"I was livid because what defined our performances at that point, and was beginning to define them more and more, was the interplay between Ritchie and myself and of course when he was sitting in the dressing room there was no interplay because I couldn't see his facial expressions! I couldn't see when he was... because we used a lot of nods and glances and winks and physical indications as to where we might go so it took a lot away. And of course I thought it was extremely bad mannered towards the audience as well, who had paid money, but still... there you go... that was Ritchie."

Ian Paice was also aware of the chemistry that was developing at the time and how important the on stage interaction was: "Each musician progresses at a different speed of course, we're all different people, but what you get is this underlying knowledge about what your partner's gonna do, you don't know what it is, but you know he's gonna do something. And there are little subliminal signals which, 2 or 3 months before you wouldn't have noticed. Sometimes you don't even hear them, it could be just an inflection of a note or it could be just a physical position it assumes."

"And so you get these incredible changes, which come from nowhere, but you all know something can happen so you - you're ready to go with it. And that's what happened. So Purple suddenly got this ability just to change direction in mid-stream, and it just seemed like it was so choreographed, but it was exactly at that moment in time because you hadn't got a preconceived idea of what it might be. That was very exciting for audiences as well as for us, because we didn't know what was gonna go next. The audience got that vibe - it was on the edge, and that was the essence of hard rock 'n' roll. We were one of the few bands that started that. It was dangerous, and exciting. And sometimes it was a train wreck, sometimes an absolute catastrophe, but when it wasn't it was exactly the opposite."

Whether or not the crowd witnessed a "train wreck" on hearing five musicians but only seeing four sadly hasn't been documented. But picturing Blackmore sitting in the dressing room as he rocked his way through the main stay of Purple's set; 'Child in Time', 'Wring That Neck' etc, it goes without saying that such behaviour didn't exactly endear him to his band mates and tension within the group soon developed. "I learnt quite early on he was going to do things for himself and no one else mattered," said Glover.

Short-changed...
Deep Purple get the blues

In 1970 Deep Purple finally broke through in its homeland with a hit single and the groundbreaking *In Rock* album. It set the seeds for the huge success that followed, but it wasn't all a bed of roses. On 4 July Purple headlined an all-day event at *The Eyrie*, home of Bedford Town Football Club, but they certainly didn't get all that they had bargained for, even though the gig created quite a deal of local press coverage at the time. No doubt it's what the promoters intended, though not all the reporting was complimentary.

It turned out to be one of the most hyped events that the town has ever witnessed. With the football club having financial difficulties someone had come up with the idea of hosting a rock concert to help raise club funds.

The hype surrounding it suggested thousands of potential fans from all over the place would descend upon the quiet shire market town.

Press reports speculated as many as twenty thousand! The football team was lucky if they got that many during an entire season so potentially it looked like a great money spinning idea. This was, after all, the golden age of rock festivals. The previous year had seen both Woodstock, and closer to home the Isle of Wight concert. Bearing this in mind it's perfectly reasonable that local residents were anxious about the show, although concerns about 'Bovver Boys' seemed grossly out of context. After all 'Bovver Boys' were more likely to be in evidence at football matches, and during

'Bovver boys' fear at pop show

PEOPLE living in Queen's Park, Bedford, are worried that skin-head "bovver boys" and layabouts will cause trouble at a "pop" concert to be held at The Eyrie in July.

The concert is being organised by Bedford Town Football Club to raise money during the close season.

Top groups like The Chicken Shack, Deep Purple and Blodwyn Pig are expected to play, supported by other groups.

Mr. Ray Capes, a director of the club, said: A number of football clubs hold concerts because they realise just how much revenue they can raise. And, of course, the Eagles need money desperately."

But a newsagent at 95 Ford End Road — near the football ground — Mr. Harold Bolton, objects so strongly to the proposal that he is organising a petition.

"I will do anything in my power to stop it", he says. "It will bring the wrong element into the area, and neither the police not the residents will be able to cope with it."

Replying to this, Mr. Capes said: "They can object to it as far as I am concerned. This is just nonsensical.

"It would be very little different from a normal match. We would make certain that we had the closest liaison with the police and the ground stewards, and there would be very careful control on people."

"It would cause us concern, because we do not like to annoy people. But we have got to exist, and running this festival would not cause the trouble these people suggest.

"In any case, how can they complain before the event is even finalised?

"Young people in Bedford pay to go to London to hear these groups. We are only trying to bring them into Bedford."

The festival will start at 2 p.m. and end at 8 p.m., Mr. Capes stresses that there will be no alcoholic drink on sale in the ground and no-one will be allowed to bring bottles into the ground.

There were mixed feelings about the plan from people living near the ground.

Mrs. Edith Kay, of 30 Nelson Street — right beside the football ground — shared Mr. Bolton's fears.

"I am sure there will be trouble", she said. "I know several people who are against this festival".

But Mrs. Zena Henwood, who has a greengrocers shop in Ford End Road, had no objections.

"We have got to realise that young people must be catered for. I don't think they will cause any trouble", she said.

● Average attendances at Eagles matches are normally about three thousand. The capacity of the ground is 18,000, but, for the concert, it will be about 20,000 because it is planned to use the pitch.

Police stand by for pop-fan invasion

ORGANISERS of to-morrow's pop festival at Bedford Town football ground are expecting a crowd of more than 10,000, but three times that number of people could flock to the town's first major open-air pop event.

Parking is going to be a major problem, and although police will have extra men on duty Inspector Richard Hodgson denied that all police leave has been cancelled.

The organisers have already sold more than 5,000 advance tickets but no one can tell how many will turn up.

Almost three times the expected 60,000 people converged on Shepton Mallet for a two-day festival last weekend, and although Bedford's bill, which includes Deep Purple and Tyrannosaurus Rex, cannot hope to attract anything like that, it is not impossible that the crowd could be 30,000.

The festival has been widely advertised, but attendance depends mainly on the weather and what else is happening. Jefferson Airplane, the American band who headlined the Shepton Mallet festival, will not now be playing a free concert in London tomorrow, and there does not appear to be a major rival attraction.

The Eagles' ground holds only 25,000 people, so what will happen if more turn up?

"We haven't reached a final decision on this," said Mr. Ray Capes, one of the football club directors.

Inspector Hodgson said that the main duties of the police will be traffic control. They have organised a oneway system, and there will be parking restrictions.

The organisers are hiring their own security people inside the grounds, and the inspector said there would be no policemen inside.

FLOP goes the pop festival

TEN thousand pop fans DIDN'T pay over £10,000 last Saturday to help out Bedford Town Football Club.

Instead, only 1,250 trickled into the Eyrie ground for the marathon 10-hour pop festival.

And the Eagles' finances remain in the same precarious state as before.

But the club have not borne the loss themselves. The sponsors, including directors of the club, have suffered instead.

They needed an attendance of 5,000 to clear themselves and last week club director Mr Ray Capes said that they had sold that much.

This week he said he was mistaken in claiming 5,000 advance tickets.

Unhappy

Mr. Capes, who refused to say what the loss to the sponsors amounted to, said that a great deal of research and three months' hard work went into organising the festival.

He put forward a number of possible reasons why the expected 10,000 did not turn up. Mr. Capes added: "We tried our best."

If the sponsors were unhappy, so were people who live near the Eyrie. Many complained about the loud music which lasted from 2 p.m. until 11.30 p.m.

But inside the ground the 1,250 clapped, shouted, and screamed for more — even when the rain came. They were very happy.

---

the soccer season this was every other weekend!

One also has to remember that although Deep Purple was headlining, the band wasn't exactly a household name when the concert was announced. The groundbreaking *In Rock* hadn't been released, nor had the accompanying single 'Black Night'. The next biggest names on the bill were Chicken Shack and Tyrannosaurus Rex, though at that time Marc Bolan's band was also considered 'underground', and it wasn't until he shortened the name and stuck on a glittering silver jacket that T. Rex became a regular on TV.

Looking at it with hindsight, perhaps it was rather ambitious to expect the fifteen to twenty thousand people that the promoters had suggested. What's more, the five thousand advanced sales that the club had claimed it had sold turned out to be a sham. Though the poor weather on the day may have deterred a few, the end result was that only 1,250 turned up. Amongst the audience was the author's brother Richard; "I don't recall much all these years on! It was my first gig and I was only fifteen. I went with a couple of mates, Bob Moore & Steve King. Kingy was the biggest fan and the instigator. I remember T. Rex was also on the bill and a local band, Satisfaction, who were very good. Deep Purple came on late. They should have been on about eleven but didn't appear until about midnight, and I remember it was very loud!"

One of the reasons Purple was late coming on was probably because the promoter was frantically trying to sort out the band's payment. Due to the poor ticket sales, he could not afford to pay them the full fee. Even after he had borrowed additional money from his brother, Purple still only wound up with half of the originally agreed fee. I guess that's why they call it the blues!

47

Plumpton Festival August 1970 - Yes, Purple!

Much has been documented on Ritchie Blackmore's stage antics at the 1970 Plumpton Festival on 9 August. Blackmore arranged for his roadie to set fire to his amps during the climactic ending to 'Mandrake Root'. Legend has it this was done because Yes had turned up late, forcing Purple to take the stage first, much to Blackmore's chagrin.

In Chris Charlesworth's biography, the first book on Purple, published in 1983, Ian Gillan said: "Yes pulled a stroke and didn't go on in time so we had to go on first. We wanted to close the show... in fact it had been agreed that we would close the show but since they weren't around we had to go on. We tried to burn the stage so that we would be the last band of the day whether Yes liked it or not."

Combined with Gillan's comments and the fact that Charlesworth actually reviewed the gig for *Melody Maker*, it would be natural to assume that was the way it happened, but is that really the true story?

The *National Jazz & Blues Festival*, to give it its full title had moved location several times over the years. Purple played the 1968 festival held at Sunbury, where its performance was all but ignored by reviewers and the audience alike. By the time it had moved to Plumpton, Purple's stature had grown considerably, following the *Concerto For Group & Orchestra* and through building up a reputation on the live circuit. For the first time in the festival's history the 1970 event was spread over four days, with Purple closing the festival on the Sunday evening.

The festival almost didn't actually happen following complaints from local residents, including the intervention of Conservative MP Martin Madden as a result of the previous year's event. This was reported in the press on the day the festival kicked off: A backlash of complaints from irate villagers is expected during the four-day pop extravaganza, which starts tonight at Plumpton Racecourse. This is the

Second Edition of Programme
All artists subject to return of contract

10th NATIONAL JAZZ, BLUES & POP MUSIC FESTIVAL **PLUMPTON** RACECOURSE Nr. LEWES, Sussex

Thursday 6th August From 7 p m	Friday 7th August From 3 p m
SOUTH OF ENGLAND SHOWCASE **Jellybread** FOX · SAMUEL PURDY CASTLE ETC · ETC	**FAMILY · GROUNDHOGS RARE BIRD · STEAMHAMMER** DADDY LONGLEGS PATTO · CLARK HUTCHINSON

TRAVEL : By road about 40 miles from London. Take A23 or A22 (A275) turning off at B2116. Special Southern Region Trains SPECIAL LATE SERVICE back to Victoria and Brighton.

Saturday 8th August From Noon
CAT STEVENS · FOTHERINGAY STRAWBS · MAGNA CARTA Granny's 'New' Intentions From Sweden MADE IN SWEDEN

☐ Evening: CHICAGO CLIMAX BLUES BAND · GRACIOUS · QUATERMASS
PETER GREEN · TASTE · KEEF HARTLEY BLACK SABBATH · JACKSON HEIGHTS · HARDIN YORK L.A. (Love Affair) · EAST OF EDEN · WILD ANGELS

ENQUIRIES : For special party rates for tickets and details of camping facilities contact the NJF Secretary at the MARQUEE 01-437 6603.

Sunday 9th August From Noon
INCREDIBLE STRING BAND From U.S.A. **TURLEY RICHARDS** Brian Davison's **EVERY WHICH WAY** From Denmark BURNIN' RED IVANHOE

☐ Evening: VAN DER GRAAF GENERATOR · WISHBONE ASH · DA DA
DEEP PURPLE · Jon Hiseman's COLOSSEUM · YES ! JUICY LUCY · CHRIS BARBER · CARAVAN · AUDIENCE FAT MATTRESS · HARD MEAT · Trevor Billmuss

FESTIVAL VILLAGE — — — Open all day to Ticketholders
Discotheque · Coffee and Snack Bar · Grocery Store
Books · Magazines · Cigarettes · Clothes · Jewellery · Oxfam Shop

48

likely result of a high court decision last week not to grant an injunction, which could have cancelled the festival. The order had been sought by Mr Martin Madden, MP for Hove, his wife and five other people living near the festival site.

Plumpton is ON — but Peter Green pulls out of the Festival

DEEP PURPLE: KEEP IT COOL!

by CHRIS CHARLESWORTH

It would have stopped the racecourse company from using the site to "cause a nuisance, damage, annoyance or disturbance to the plaintiffs."

A festival official said, "it is certainly possible that we will get many more complaints than ever before. Although the great majority of residents seem to be behind us, there are still a hard core who are bitter about the High Court decision." The official added, "We are doing everything possible this year to avoid complaints. And those we do get will probably be completely unjustified." The security force hired to keep order at the festival has been doubled this year to more than 200 and a large fresh water main has been laid to the festival site. Large numbers of additional toilets have also been provided. Thousands more are expected by tomorrow night, when the main festival begins. "This has all the makings of a big one," a spokesman from the organisers said hopefully.

PLUMPTON IS ON—but Peter Green's eagerly-awaited debut at the N.J.F.'s Jazz and Blues Festival this weekend is off. Peter told me this week that contrary to the belief he would not be playing on the Saturday night festival session.

"I have chickened out and told the organisers I will not be playing after all, he said. "I just don't want to do it."

It was to have been Pete's first public appearance since he quit Fleetwood Mac earlier this year. The artists who are playing appealed this week to the fans to behave themselves after the hassle the organisers have had in the High Court over the injunction brought to stop the Festival.

ROGER CHAPMAN, singer with Family, declared "I am really pleased the festival is going on as planned. Now the responsibility rests with the crowds and ourselves to make sure things work.

IAN PAICE, drummer with Deep Purple, said "The news that the festival is on is just great. I just hope now that everyone has a good time and aren't any hassles. If the crowds behave it will show those who were ..."

"Several Sussex bands, including Jellybread, are featured tonight in the "South Of England Showcase" concert opener. Tomorrow Family and The Groundhogs top the bill and on Saturday Cat Stevens and Peter Green, late of Fleetwood Mac, are the big attractions. The festival ends on Sunday, with the Incredible String Band, Colosseum, Yes and Deep Purple."

As mentioned in the press report, the first day (Thursday) kicked off with the showcase for local bands and as such it only attracted a limited audience. The Jazz element of the festival had by and large disappeared by 1970. Colosseum could be construed to have some jazz content, but Chris Barber was the only jazz act on the whole bill. By 1970 the event consisted mainly of rock bands, and several blues acts. Although the festival was marketed as a Blues Mecca, there were none of the overseas performers that had appeared at earlier bashes. In fact there hadn't been an overseas artist of note since 1967.

The festival program confirms the running order with Yes scheduled to go on before Purple. It also shows that *Vertigo* signings Juicy Lucy had been earmarked to close the festival on the Sunday evening. Yes and Juicy Lucy were allocated forty-five minute sets while Purple had the longest set of the entire weekend with a full seventy-five minutes.

The *UK Rock Festivals* website includes recollections from people who attended the show. There are also photos on the site, including rather grainy images of both Purple and Yes.

One recollection posted on the website by a chap who merely refers to himself as 'Spike' recalls, "I was actually employed as a part time security guard. Job entailed no more than guarding a jump fence or hurdle overnight to stop punters from dismantling them for firewood. Luckily the stage was set across the inner part of the course - backstage one side and punters the other. The chaps that were guarding the peoples end had all sorts of problems apparently, but I was at back stage end and spent a very peaceful time. Maybe my memory is going but I do seem to remember Deep Purple setting fire to the stage because the organisers wouldn't let them play on into Juicy Lucy's slot although they hadn't turned up. I'm probably wrong on this score, but the rumour on the street at the time gave this as one reason for the festival moving to Reading."

With the concerns prior to the festival kicking off, if 'Spike' is correct, Blackmore's antics were responsible for the festival becoming synonymous with Reading for evermore! But it's the comments

PROGRAMME

Friday 7th August

VILLAGE		ARENA	
Noon - 3.00	D.J. Session	3.00 - 4.00	Daddy Longlegs
		4.00 - 4.45	Patto
		4.45 - 5.30	Clark-Hutchinson
		5.30 - 6.30	AUDIENCE
		6.30 - 7.00	D.J.
		7.00 - 7.45	Rare Bird
		7.45 - 8.30	Fat Mattress
		8.30 - 9.15	Groundhogs
		9.15 - 10.00	Steamhammer
		10.00 - 11.00	FAMILY

Saturday 8th August

VILLAGE		ARENA	
		12.00 - 12.45	Made in Sweden
		12.45 - 1.30	Gracious
		1.30 - 2.14	Fotheringay
		2.15 - 3.15	Cat Stevens
		3.15 - 4.00	Strawbs
4.00 - 4.45	T2	4.00 - 4.45	Magna Carta
4.45 - 5.30	Brethren	4.45 - 5.30	Granny's 'New' Intentions
		5.30 - 6.30	EAST OF EDEN
6.30 - 7.30	Wild Angels	6.30 - 7.15	Peter Green
7.30 - 8.30	Quatermass	7.15 - 8.00	Keef Hartley
		8.00 - 8.45	Black Sabbath
8.30 - 9.30	Chicago Climax Blues Band	8.45 - 9.30	Jackson Heights
		9.30 - 10.15	Hardin York
		10.15 - 11.15	TASTE

Sunday 9th August

VILLAGE		ARENA	
		12.00 - 12.45	Burnin' Red Ivanhoe
		12.45 - 1.30	Matthews Southern Comfort
		1.30 - 2.00	Trevor Billmuss
		2.00 - 3.00	INCREDIBLE STRING BAND
		3.00 - 3.30	Turley Richards
3.30 - 4.30	Caravan	3.30 - 4.15	Chris Barber Band
4.30 - 5.30	Wishbone Ash	4.15 - 5.15	Every Which Way
		5.15 - 6.15	COLOSSEUM
		6.15 - 6.45	D.J.
6.30 - 7.30	Chris Barber Band	6.45 - 7.30	Van der Graaf Generator
7.30 - 8.30	Da-Da	7.30 - 8.15	Hard Meat
		8.15 - 9.00	Yes!
		9.00 - 10.15	DEEP PURPLE
		10.15 - 11.00	Juicy Lucy

about Juicy Lucy that help to establish the true story behind Blackmore's antics.

Further evidence that Purple actually performed after Yes comes from another eye-witness, Andrew Harris: "Yes played at around 7.30 on the Sunday in chilly but clear weather and people took the wooden chairs from the press area and made a bonfire about 30 yards back from the stage. Jon Andersen was in great voice and the evening turned into one of those glad to be alive experiences."

Harris was clearly a Yes fan, so had they been upstaged by Blackmore's pyromania, I am sure it would have left a negative memory, even thirty odd years later. Another recollection of the show comes from an Israeli student, Albert: "Deep Purple gave their 'Black Night' its premiere then and as usual, put one or two speakers on fire." This recollection isn't wholly accurate. 'Black Night' wasn't premiered at Plumpton, indeed it had already been in the set for quite some time before this gig. Neither contrary to popular belief did Blackmore set fire to his speakers as a matter of course. In fact it was only at prestigious gigs such as this that he made a concerted effort to make an explosive impression.

Of course what has been documented, was the visual impact that Purple's performance had on the press. Charlesworth wrote in *Melody Maker*: *Blackmore set upon his stack with the rage of an executioner. It caught fire and was then hurled across the stage into the crowd. Guitars were flung around the stage in wild abandon. Jon Lord's organ rocked like a boat in a storm as the strobe lighting flashed.*

Shortly after the event Blackmore commented, "I get very annoyed when I get on stage and find I can't play. That happens quite a lot, like at Plumpton. I couldn't do anything that night. The guitar kept going out of tune and a freezing wind was ripping across the stage. That's why I set my amp on fire."

Getting back to the saga involving Juicy Lucy, they had recently acquired a new guitarist; none other than Micky Moody, who of course went on to help establish David Coverdale's solo career and become a mainstay of Whitesnake's early years. Moody's memories of the story about Juicy Lucy failing to turn up are as follows: "To my recollection, Yes were the penultimate act, but as the show was running late they took Juicy Lucy's spot. Deep Purple's powers that be then muscled in and grabbed the following (and final) spot denying us an appearance. We were disappointed, to put it mildly!"

So although Moody's recollections aren't a hundred per cent accurate, they do also confirm that Purple did actually go on after Yes, just as the program intended, and dispels the story that Gillan had regaled over a decade after the event.

Who was Deep Purple's second guitarist?

If this question was asked in a pub quiz, most people would probably answer, Tommy Bolin, the young American, formerly of the James Gang who replaced Blackmore in 1975, recording one album, *Come Taste The Band*, and completing one world tour, before the band took an eight year hiatus. However it would not be inaccurate to refer to Tommy Bolin as the sixth guitarist to *play* with Purple! Prior to appointing Bolin, the band spent a couple of days auditioning the ex-Humble Pie player Clem Clempson.

Three years earlier during a North American tour, Blackmore took ill with hepatitis and the band initially decided to continue with a replacement. Spirit guitarist Randy California, did one show in Quebec before they decided to cancel the rest of the tour. However before the gig with California they had also rehearsed with Al Kooper of Blood, Sweat And Tears, who decided he couldn't go through with it. But the actual second guitarist to play with Purple was two years before that incident.

Just over two weeks after the Plumpton Festival, Purple was touring the States, where they rocked up in San Antonio, Texas on 28 August 1970. Deep Purple's gig that night was at a venue called the Jam Factory. It was the band's first US tour with the MKII line-up. They had performed the *Concerto For Group & Orchestra* three days earlier at the Hollywood Bowl but with the band's popularity having already dropped off since the success of 'Hush' two years earlier, they struggled to get other gigs.

The original date printed on the tickets was 21st August but for some unexplained reason it was changed to 28th. The band was also booked to play two shows: at 7 pm & 11 pm. Before the second show could start, Ritchie Blackmore collapsed. Feeling unwell he wasn't in sufficient health to perform. However all was not lost, as there happened to be another guitarist willing to step up to the plate. None other than Christopher Cross, who years later became a well-respected and successful singer songwriter!

In an interview, Christopher Cross said, "One night Deep Purple came to San Antonio. First night of the tour again. Ritchie Blackmore got sick from a flu shot and couldn't perform. But the show was sold out at a place called the Pussycat Club (sic), which was a big club that I'd played. Eric Johnson played there as well with his original band called Mariani. And Billy Gibbons used to have a band called Moving Sidewalk, and before they were ZZ they used to play there. But I subbed for Blackmore. They didn't want to cancel the show so they told people Blackmore wasn't going to be there, but I was kind of a local hero, and I was going to sit in, in his place and if people wanted to stay, they could stay. About 80% of the people stayed. And so I played guitar for Deep Purple. Then when they were leaving at the airport I got to meet Ritchie, and he gave me his pick."

In the interview Cross was also asked what's it like to be 19 and suddenly on stage as Deep Purple's guitarist? "It was exciting but almost embarrassing. I realised I had no business being up there sitting in for Ritchie Blackmore, but the guy who owned the club wanted the show to go on. Jon Lord and the band wanted the show to go on. The singer wasn't happy about it as I remember, but you know I was just jumping in there, and I realised how ridiculous it was that I would be subbing for Ritchie. But it was exciting. I was a big fan of Ritchie's, a huge fan of his playing so I knew the hits, and I knew a lot of the big things, but then we just jammed some blues and stuff like that. And the guys just tried to have a good time with it. It was their very first tour in the States and they didn't want to cancel (the gig) and have that be the way they started. It's hard to remember but it was pretty heady. It was just really exciting to meet, as a guitarist, artists who were these huge heroes of mine."

With Cross's memory, hazy and his misplaced recollection that it was at the Pussycat Club, the author contacted him via his website. The Webmaster replied: "Interestingly enough, Christopher had also begun to think maybe he imagined this night. It happened in the early 1970s (he's not sure of the year). But recently, CC was playing in Austin and, after the show, a guy came up to him and said he was part of the opening act (Mariani) and he had lots of memories of the evening. So, apparently, it really did happen. It was obviously a last minute deal and only once, so it's understandable that they could all kind of forget about it."

An interview with Eric Johnson, then the budding guitarist with

Mariani sheds further light on the story. When asked what his favourite Mariani gig was, Johnson replied: "We played a couple of gigs down in San Antonio. There used to be this place called Jam Factory. We opened for Deep Purple down there. It's where I met Chris Geppert (Christopher Cross) actually. He was filling in for Ritchie Blackmore that night because Ritchie was in the hospital, sick, and Chris knew Joe Miller who was putting on the show and Chris knew every single Deep Purple song backwards and forwards. So Chris shows up with this crazy huge hair and a big beard and a Flying V! Just totally different than what he was like later. He was really a hard rocker and he wanted to play through my *Marshall* with Deep Purple. I remember at the time, I told him 'you have to use channel 2 'cos channel 1 is broken' and he looked at me like I was just saying that to goof him up, but it was really true. That was a fond memory and a great gig. We got to open for Deep Purple and because Ritchie was sick they went on really late, so we got to play way longer than we were supposed to and the crowd loved us! It was fun. It was just a really magical night, then we got asked to come and play Jam Factory again. That band had a lot of potential. We only played a handful of gigs but there was a real magic to it that people responded to."

In another, more recent interview, this time with Greg Prato in 2013, Cross reiterated: "I had a promoter friend named Joe Miller who I did a lot of gopher work for and stuff like that. I had a local band, and he was kind of managing me at the time. Joe was promoting the Deep Purple show at a place called the Jam Factory. It was their very first show in the United States ever (*sic*), and someone advised them to get flu shots. They did, and Ritchie Blackmore got very sick.

They didn't want to cancel the show if they could help it, and Joe said, 'You know, there's this guitarist in town who's a big fan of Ritchie's and he could probably step in'. The singer was in favour of it, I remember, but Joe pretty much ran the band and was the one that made the decision that it was better to play than not play. So I came down. I had a Flying V and long hair, and I'm this big Ritchie fan. We played the songs that I knew and then we jammed some blues. They told the crowd Ritchie wouldn't be there. It was a great moment for me.

Then when they left town I went to the airport and got to meet Ritchie and he thanked me for covering for him. He was cool. But what's funny is, *Eagle Rock Records*, which released *Doctor Faith*, my last album in 2011, they have Deep Purple on the label. So I asked Max Vaccaro, who runs the label, if he mentioned the story to Jon Lord. He did, and Jon Lord said that never happened, ever."

Blackmore soon recovered and was well enough to continue the tour. Cross went on to establish his career as a singer songwriter, best known for his Top Ten hits, 'Sailing', 'Ride like the Wind', and 'Arthur's Theme (Best That You Can Do)'.

'Cos everyone calls you Big E

When *In Rock* was released the sleeve credits listed chief roadie as Ian (Bige) Hansford. Hansford hailed from Warrington in Cheshire but had moved south and roadied for The Maze, which is how he was originally brought in to the Deep Purple fold.

The nickname Bige was established after Glover and Gillan had joined. Prior to that, with two Ian's as part of the set-up, Paice was referred to as Little Ian, and Hansford as Big Ian. With the arrival of Gillan, to help differentiate between the three Ian's, the new vocalist took Hansford's previous moniker. Little Ian and Big Ian's names were often abbreviated to the first syllable of their names so whilst Gillan was now Big Ian or Big "E", Hansford, also Big "E" had the pronunciation of his name changed to By-ge, which was duly spelt Bige. So now you know!

Maybe it would have been less confusing for all if he had kept the other nickname that he had also acquired during Purple's first year together - The Warrington Ape - a comment on his stature and place of origin!

Deep Purple Equals No.

An unlikely confrontation occurred in 1970 when The Equals, who included guitarist and future solo artist Eddy Grant, claimed that Deep Purple was copying them. The Equals' style was a long way from Deep Purple's, as their sixties hits such as 'Baby, Come Back' and 'Viva Bobby Joe' clearly showed. But with Purple suddenly hitting the UK charts with 'Black Night', and drawing popularity from mere pop fans, as well as the underground movement, something clearly stuck in the Equals' craw. Purple found it so amusing that they decided to send the band up at their shows.

At the Fairfield Halls, Croydon on 22 November the show started differently than normal with Ian Gillan declaring, "We're going to do an Equals' number." This comical little ditty consisted of Ian Gillan yodelling over a light-hearted accompaniment. It normally lasted for around ninety seconds before ripping in to 'Speed King'.

Shortly after the concert Gillan said, "I suppose it was a bit silly saying that. It's best just to ignore those sort of things. But I'm just sick to death of all the snobbery that's going on. It seems you are only underground if you are completely underground."

Over the next few months the band continued to open shows with "their Equals' No." although on a couple of occasions during a European tour in April '71 it was followed by a drum solo. Even in the musical freedom of the seventies that may seem like an odd way to start a gig, although it was out of necessity. At both the Montreux Casino, Switzerland and a week later at the Vejlby-Risskov Hallen in Århus, Denmark, just as the first chords of 'Speed King' were played the power failed. Before the roadies could sort it out Ian Paice quickly improvised with a drum solo.

Whilst it was all deemed as fun by Purple, the situation was far from comical for Eddy Grant who aged only 23 suffered a heart attack and had to leave the band. Purple continued to flourish, The Equals continued for several years and Grant recovered and went on to establish a successful solo career so everything turned out equal in the end!

Band banned

As Purple's live reputation grew following the recruitment of Ian Gillan and Roger Glover to the band, so did the atmosphere at the gigs. During the band's UK tour in early 1971 such was the enthusiasm of the audiences that Purple found itself banned from several venues including the Brighton Dome and Manchester's Free Trade Hall, necessitating alternative venues in the respective towns and cities.

One of the problems arose from heavy-handed bouncers who seemed intent on spoiling the fun that some audience members derived from dancing, or 'freaking out' as it was referred to in those days. Anyone who has seen the awesome footage of the band performing 'Mandrake Root' at London's Queen Elizabeth Hall filmed by *London Weekend Television* will know what that means as two females move to the music, oblivious to all around them.

Ian Gillan put it into context when he spoke with *Disc & Music Echo* in March '71. He explained what they encountered when the band arrived at one of the venues. "A bouncer said to us, quite proudly, that he'd thrown someone out the week before - for dancing! We had a little word with him but there was still someone walking up and down the middle aisle while we were playing, patting people on the head to make sure they didn't get too excited. So I said to the crowd: 'There's someone being very bolshie down there, everyone look at him.' And 2,000 heads stared at him. He really cringed and then disappeared. We didn't see him again."

Run-ins with bouncers seemed all too common on the tour and tensions between them and the band were at breaking point. "We were considering doing amazing things to them if they really got out of hand," explained Gillan. "Ritchie was quite prepared to smash his best guitar over someone's mouth. And I got to the point where I was making up my mind which end of the mic' stand to use on somebody. It's not as if audiences want to smash up places. And even if they smash a couple of chairs so what! We'd pay for it all. All they want to do is dance a bit and enjoy themselves.

At Croydon's Fairfield Halls the previous year, where they had performed their 'Equals' Number' for the first time, apparently a balcony nearly collapsed as a result of the collective movement from enthusiastic fans. "The other halls used this as an excuse to ban us," said Gillan.

Ian Gillan's weird animals
and big blonde giants!

Whilst still a member of Episode Six and following encouragement by Roger Glover, Ian Gillan started writing. "When I was in Episode Six with Roger he wrote and I said I wished I could and he went mad. He really got angry and told me that anyone could write, it was just a matter of sitting down and doing it. He was fed up with people telling him they wished they could write like him."

During this period Gillan started writing - not just songs, but poems. A collection of his poems written in 1969 was later published as *The Candy Horizon*. One of them entitled *Grabsplatter* was also adopted for an instrumental recorded for a BBC radio session. Around the same time he also started a children's fantasy story. By the end of 1970, having been in Purple for just over a year he commented, "I've just written a children's story called *Cherkazoo*. It's a fantasy with weird animals and big blonde giants and things." The report in *Disc & Music Echo* quoted Gillan as saying, "I went to see Richard Harris (sic) and Stanley Baker at their offices and they were interested enough to consider filming it for television next Christmas."

Welsh actor Baker, perhaps best known for his role in the 1964 film *Zulu*, had by then also ventured in to producing. By the time Ian Gillan met with Baker he had already become a founding member and director of Independent TV channel Harlech. Fellow directors included Richard Burton and Elizabeth Taylor. Burton was a close friend of Baker's and it's probably he rather than Harris who was in attendance at the meeting.

"It's taken two years on and off to write," explained Gillan. "I find writing very relaxing. It's great when you sit down with a big blank sheet of paper and you begin to fill it with words. I wrote about anything - take *Monty Python*, I'm sure a lot of that comes from what happens in the studio. You can sit in a pub and say to a friend 'Can you imagine if this happened?' and you build a big thing out of it. You could write it all down and get a story. I sit down at home and create fantasises and write about them."

With Purple's hectic touring and recording schedule there was little time for Gillan to devote too much attention to the *Cherkazoo* project, but in September 1972 he found time to go into the studio and lay down some songs to go alongside any potential film. In fact the same year, probably following a break in touring after a US tour was cancelled when Blackmore contracted hepatitis, Gillan had produced the one and only album by British band Jerusalem. But they soon split, and bassist Paul Dean, drummer Ray Sparrow and guitarist Bob Cooke formed a new band called Pussy. Gillan also produced their recordings but only a single was released. The rest eventually saw the light of day in 2011.

But back to *Cherkazoo* and with the help of Glover and Lord, alongside other musicians such as guitarist Ray Fenwick a few songs were completed and some were pressed up on acetates, although the label mistakenly referred to it as Chez Kazoo. The songs remained unreleased until 1992 when some of them appeared on the album *Cherkazoo & Other Stories* - the rest of the album being made up of 1974 recordings rejected by *Purple Records* for Gillan's debut solo album (see page 87). A part of the film script is available to read on Gillan's website.

Emidisc

CHEZ KAZOO

WHAT'S NEW FINNIGAN

Although Gillan's original plans for a full-scale production never materialised, a musical based around the songs and ideas was performed by the *Axe Valley Rock Music Society* at the Guildhall in Axminster, Devon over four days in September 1999. This incredibly low key production by Steve Black was put together with Ian Gillan's help. As well as using some of the songs from the original *Cher Kazoo* project, additional pieces by Black and Gillan were also incorporated throughout the ten scenes spread over two acts.

Axminster is more famous for producing carpets than musicals, but it's fair to say that with Gillan's personal involvement he certainly didn't pull the rug from under the *Axe Valley Rock Music Society*! And if you think that's bad, let's remember that some of the original recordings from the project still remain unreleased and would appear to have been swept under the carpet!

And you've not been
hit by flying cushions...

O ne of the most unusual occurrences ever at a Deep Purple gig happened at the short-lived Brighton venue Big Apple on 27 February 1971. Originally called the Regent Dance Hall it was constructed in an arched superstructure on the roof of the Regent Cinema and was opened in December 1923. It had a capacity for 1,500 dancers on its specially sprung floor. Its popularity had declined by the 1960s and in July 1967 the dance hall was closed and converted into a bingo hall. It was reopened as the Big Apple in late 1970.

Although it was essentially a dance hall, more often than not in those days fans would sit down at rock gigs. The Big Apple however went further than most non-seated venues by supplying large cushions to sit on and it soon became customary for the audiences to have cushion fights towards the end of the show. Apparently at T.Rex's gig in December 1970 it prompted Marc Bolan to say, "Gee man, you hippies are dangerous."

On the day of Purple's Big Apple gig Jon Lord did an interview with Richard Green for *New Musical Express*, after which he drove the journalist to the venue. Green recounted in his article published the following week, *we arrived to find the gigantic club absolutely packed.* This was a reflection on Purple's growing popularity following the previous year's success with the hit single 'Black Night' and the *In Rock* album. The follow up single 'Strange Kind of Woman' was released a couple of weeks before the show and actually entered the UK chart on the day of this gig.

Green continued his report by saying, *the two-hour plus set was nothing short of amazing. The crowd was almost hysterical in its acclaim and after the encores - 'Black Night' and 'Lucille' - the stage was three feet deep in cushions. It should be explained that cushion throwing is a sign of approval at this particular venue and no malice is intended.*

Brighton's cushion throwing ended the following month after the venue put on its last gig, and three years later the building was demolished.

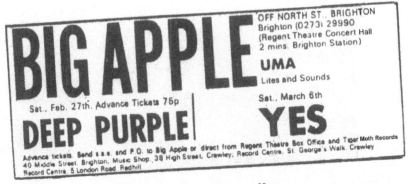

Strange Kind Of Fireball

The recording for *Fireball* started in September 1970 at London's De Lane Lea Studios in Kingsway. However due to the continual bout of gigging, largely bought on by the success of *In Rock*, only one track was laid down at this session. Thus the country flavoured 'Anyone's Daughter' has the dubious honour of being the first new recording since the band had finished sessions for the previous album with 'Black Night'.

The group then decided to spend a couple of weeks at the end of the year writing new songs and the plan was to spend January recording the album. In December, after a hectic bout of touring they locked themselves away for a fortnight in a remote farmhouse in Devon, though little progress was made. The band was exhausted from the recent spate of work and spent most of the time in the local pubs, and in Blackmore's case, indulging in one of his favourite past times, séances. Friction within the band also started to play a part around this time and petty in-wrangling often disrupted the work.

Purple People

Deep Purple took a house in Devon – and were tucked away down in the countryside for over a month working on their new album.

First, however, they took a fortnight's holiday over Christmas, and then made swift trips to Amsterdam and Rotterdam.

And then it was down to the West Country – with Ritchie taking his wife Babs, and Jon Lord his wife Judy and their young daughter Sara.

"We thought it would be nice to cut ourselves off completely," says Roger Glover, "so that we could work away at new material without any distractions at all."

Deep Purple are at present on a nationwide tour of Britain, which they are planning to follow with another two-month tour of the States.

This next LP will be Deep Purple's sixth, their last being incredibly successful "Deep Purple In Rock", which stayed in the top end of the LP charts for months on end.

"We're still very proud of that album," says Roger, "because it showed where we were at that time. It was a stand . . . not a collection of bits and pieces and other people's songs, but our music at that point in time.

"We're still the same band, but we've moved on since then. In the next album we'll be stretching out a bit, and the music will have slightly more variation."

The relationship between Blackmore and Gillan started to take a turn for the worse, and the singer later admitted his drinking was getting the better of him during this period. But an even bigger friction developed that has been less well documented; one that almost resulted in the departure of one of the founding members. "There was an awful argument that came during the writing sessions for what became *Fireball*", explained Lord to the author in 2007. "We were down in Devon and my wife had just had a baby. I drove back in the middle of some writing sessions overnight, before the M5 existed - horrendous journey. I picked up my wife and baby then drove them right back down again back into writing sessions, 24-36 hours later, my new baby got a terrible cold because this place we were in was damp and awful. My wife just threw a wobbler and said, 'I've got to go back to London'. So I drove her back again and then drove back down again, thus missing two or three days of the writing sessions. They were not happy about that and rightly so, although perhaps they could have been a bit kinder given the circumstances. A big argument blew up about that and I threatened to quit for some strange reason but of course it was just one of those moments: 'oh fuck it I'm going to leave' and walked out and slammed the door."

Fortunately Lord quickly changed his mind, and as 1970 was drawing to a close, Glover commented that he hoped the album would be released by March. As it turned out, by this time only a handful of tracks had been written. Amongst these were a number called 'I'm Alone' and a song about a prostitute, 'Strange Kind Of Woman'. These were coupled together and released in February with the latter as the a-side. It certainly kept the band in the eye of the rock fraternity, while the rest of the album was still to be put together. 'Strange Kind Of Woman' followed 'Black Night' into the top ten and helped to reinforce Purple as a major force to be reckoned with.

In 1995 in an interview with Neil Jeffries, Blackmore said, "We booked some studio time and arranged to meet. When I got there we were all there but Jon. I phoned the office and said: 'Look, the four of us are here and ready

Deep Purple's great new single
'Strange kind of woman' is now available on [EMI] Harvest HAR 5033

E.M.I. RECORDS (THE GRAMOPHONE CO. LTD.), E.M.I. HOUSE, 20 MANCHESTER SQUARE, LONDON.

but there's no sign of Jon'. 'Oh, he's here', they said. 'What's he doing in London, he should be here to write and record? Put him on.' 'I, er, I had some things to do. Carry on without me, you don't need me to be there.' So we did. We sat around and came up with 'Strange Kind Of Woman', and after we'd recorded it I remember Paicey coming over to me and saying: 'You don't think Jon is going to expect his name on the writing credits for that, is he?' And I said: 'I'll bet he does, why not ask him?' Sure enough, he did - he insisted on it! I couldn't really take him seriously after that."

As the recording sessions progressed Ian Paice made a startling discovery whilst walking around the studio. Roger Glover documented this at the time; "Ian Paice was walking around carrying his snare drum and hitting it. As he walked from the studio area into the corridor on his way to the control room, he noticed the change in sound of his snare drum. It was so dramatic that he called us all in and demonstrated the difference between the quiet 'toc' of the drum in the soundproofed, padded and baffled studio, and the resounding crash of the drum in the corridor, bringing out the full range of sound... the real sound, exciting and loud! From that point to the end of the making of *Fireball*, Ian set his drums up in the corridor, greatly inconveniencing everybody, but getting such a good sound that we all forgave him."

Recording sessions continued to be fitted into the tight schedule as and when, at both De Lane Lea and at Olympic studios, just south of the River Thames in Barnes. Yet by May even the record companies were getting impatient. Particularly in America where the band was scheduled to tour in July, and *Warner Bros* desperately needed

Deep Purple do themselves really proud

DEEP PURPLE: ✳ Strange Kind Of Woman (Harvest) says much for Deep Purple that, despite the large number of groups currently churning out heavy music, it has ill managed to develop a distinctive sound of its own.

This latest single again generates the outfit's own particular brand hard rock — yet, for all its earthiness and thickness, it's noteworthy the tight performance and quality of musicianship.

✳ **TIPPED FOR CHARTS**
† **CHART POSSIBLE**

The beat is penetrating and compelling, the vocal is spirited and gutsy, and the guitars are pungent and reverberating. The melody line is little more than a repetitive riff — which, let's face it, is the basis of all pure rock.

Midway through the set, there's an unexpected slow passage of considerable delicacy that's effective because of its sharp contrast from the remainder of the routine. Another good one from Purple, which should do the lads proud.

a new album to promote on the back of the tour. A couple of weeks of solid studio work were set aside for early June, yet still the album wasn't complete! As such *Warner Bros* decided to release the album by including the single 'Strange Kind Of Woman'. To pacify impatient fans awaiting a new album in the UK, Ian Gillan promised that when the album would be released it would include an extended version of the track.

His comments appeared to be borne out of criticism the band was receiving from some quarters for releasing singles. David Hughes of *Disc* magazine questioned how Purple could be progressive and have hit singles. Gillan retorted by denying the band was progressive, "We're a rock band, we like to play good stuff and we think about what we do. But if you are successful then it becomes popular. The singles market can obviously help your success. But we don't set out to make singles, we just put one out if we happen to come

Deep Purple—Fireball (Warner Bros.)

Deep Purple was a remarkable band of musicians back when they were doing "Hush." Now two and a half years and one Royal Philharmonic later, they are even better. Ian Gillan, fresh from his performance in the title role of "Jesus Christ, Superstar," is a lead vocalist with presence, and his five cohorts give him solid backing all the way without surrendering their individual instrumental personalities. It all makes

for a rare cohesiveness. "Anyone's Daughter" is probably the most entertaining cut on the record, at least as much for its good-natured self-derision as for the sheer countryesque joy of its delivery. "Strange Kind Of Woman" is infectious rock 'n' roll at its best and there are five other selections, any one of which could easily become someone's personal favorite. This is more than just a good album—it's a quality album.

ALBUMS

AND REVIEW SERVICE ★ DISC PULL-OUT CHARTS

'Fireball' Purple burn off their imitators

DEEP PURPLE have the disadvantage of having to live up to a reputation, but they'll have no worries with "Fireball" (Harvest SHVL 793, £2.29). They also have to keep up a stream of good sounds, while fending off attempts by other groups to pick their brains and musical originality. They'll manage that too.

With the exception of one track, "Fireball" is undiluted, funky Purple. The exception, a sad inclusion to an otherwise extremely good album, is "Anyone's Daughter." Ian Gillan's vocals aren't really suitable for Dylanesque talking blues, and as the words come close to banal, the whole number just comes over as a send up. If it was intended as such, it seems an awful waste of time and effort.

Now for the good news, and that's the remaining six tracks. While they are different in musical and lyrical content, they have kept an identifiable theme running through with strong organ and bass lines from Jon Lord and Roger Glover. For arrangement and all over goodness, "Fools" is half a head in front. Emotive searing words are fitted to a tight drum/guitar accompaniment, with a plaintive organ backing soaring through it all.

Again with the accent on the words, "No One Came" follows a close second. It has quiet, maracca shuffling passages making a foil for the heavy noises thundering in for maximum effect. The songs all seem rather bitter-sweet, but create good feelings all the same.

Quality—very good. Value for money—yes, definitely.

up with something suitable. It's got to be commercial, and not too extended. That way we don't compromise. There'll be a longer version of 'Strange Kind Of Woman' on the next album. And LPs are more important to us because you can live longer with album success."

As it was, ironically the US version of the album released that July

DEEP PURPLE — STRANGE KIND OF A WOMAN — (Warner Bros.)

It's commercial. A little long. Probably be a hit. Except for that little 3/4 time break it gets on it and stays on it.

turned out to include a slightly longer take than had been released on the single, with a lengthier guitar fade out. When the LP finally saw the light of day in Europe in September, exactly a year after it had been started, Ian Gillan's promise of an extended version of 'Strange Kind Of Woman' never materialised. 'Demon's Eye', the last track to be written and recorded was included at the behest of this track. As such America, Canada and Japan were the only countries to release the album with a 20 seconds longer 'Strange Kind Of Woman'.

As it turned out, *Fireball* was originally released a month before the first releases on the bands' own *Purple Records* label. Ironic really, as the company's advertising slogan was 'The Open Ear' and the album was the most adventurous this line-up produced. The majority of the band regarded it as too left field, but the fans loved it and *Fireball* was the band's first UK number one.

Lay Down, Baby Face, Stay Down

D eep Purple had an unexpected rest in autumn 1971 after Ian Gillan contracted hepatitis, necessitating cancellation of an American tour in October. With some spare time on their hands, Ritchie Blackmore and Ian Paice went into the studio to experiment with some ideas along with Thin Lizzy's Phil Lynott, with the view of possibly starting a new band. "What Ritchie and Ian Paice wanted to do was a Jimi Hendrix type thing. I can't remember if it was before or after but they also had a rehearsal at Hanwell with Hamish Stuart from the Average White Band. I can vaguely remember one rehearsal at Hanwell and then once in the studio with Phil Lynott," recalls Ian Hansford.

Some sources suggest Ritchie had originally wanted to have Paul Rodgers as the vocalist for these sessions; such was his admiration for the Free front man, but there is no evidence to back this up. But in light of the fact that he wanted to produce a more blues based sound to suit a vocalist of Rodgers style goes some way to explain why he was now looking at Ian Gillan's singing in a different light.

Blackmore had visions of a Jimi Hendrix Experience type band. Lynott, the young half-Irish, half-Afro-Guyanese bassist-cum-vocalist, had caught Blackmore's eye. Lynott and Thin Lizzy had moved to London earlier in the year to further its career, releasing its eponymous debut album in April.

While Gillan recuperated at home, Blackmore, Paice and Lynott worked together on some ideas at the Music Centre in Wembley on 22nd November. Blackmore spoke about it in the late nineties: "We made a couple of tapes. The ex-management has them. They were not finished and there were only three songs, half-finished."

In fact it was two instrumental takes and one full version with guitar overdubs and solo, plus vocals of a Blackmore tune. Judging from Lynott's lyrics, an educated guess suggests the song could have been called 'Wanted Alive' but the song was just filed under the project name of Baby Face. Although the recordings remain unreleased, the riff materialised two years later as 'Lay Down, Stay Down'.

Some rumours also abound that Baby Face did a version of Edgar Winter's 'Dying To Live', not recorded by his brother Johnny, as has previously been documented in Purple literature. But given that Winter's song, released the same year on his second album *White Trash* is a piano based ballad, it's hard to imagine the trio working up a version of it.

In May '72 Blackmore did say, "We have got a couple of tracks down and I am pretty pleased with them. It's coming on very slowly but I want to be sure about it. It's a sort of rock/blues band, very different from Purple. I would like to make a single with them because that's the quickest way to get

Ritchie is taking his time over his solo project which may reach fruition by Christmas. Already he has written material which is not for Purple, and made tapes with Ian Paice at the drums and a bassist/vocalist from another group who wishes to remain nameless.

"It's coming on very slowly, but I want to be sure about it. It's a sort of rock/blues band, very different from Purple. I would like to make a single with them because that's the quickest way to get things going, but they wouldn't play our kind of stuff on the radio.

"We have got a couple of tracks down and I am pretty pleased with them. I want to do something where it is all my own fault if it goes wrong, or my own fault if it turns out good.

"After Christmas it may be the turning point for Purple. We are having a good time but it's got to end sometime. Jon is doing his own things and Roger is into production.

"I just think there is room for more excitement in today's music and I want to do something about it. I think I can do something more exciting than Deep Purple."

"Although we are all good musicians in Purple, we are limited to certain things. It's hard to write hard riffs all the time.

"I don't think we can get much bigger than we are at the moment and it's a nice position to be in. But it can't last for ever."

things going, but they wouldn't play our kind of stuff on the radio. I want to do something where it is all my own fault if it goes wrong, or my own fault if it turns out good. I just think there is room for more excitement in today's music and I want to do something about it. I think I can do something more exciting than Deep Purple. I want to get on with my band - we all want to get on with our other interests - and I have to envisage an end to Deep Purple to stay sane. But we'll keep together for a bit yet because we're earning good money and we might as well clean up - I think we deserve it. I starved for six years, and the band has built itself a good reputation over the years."

As it was Ritchie stayed with Purple for three more years and as Thin Lizzy's career took off, the project with Lynott never progressed. Blackmore described it as having more of a Hendrix sound than Purple, "because Phil sang that way," he said. "We were going to form a band with the three of us. It was when I wanted to leave Deep Purple, and then Ian Paice asked why and I said: 'I can't work with Ian Gillan.' In the end they went my way. That's what happened when Roger and Ian went. And Ian Paice, Phil and me had been working together cause I wanted to do a bit more bluesy music. But then we had new guys in the band and songs like 'Mistreated'. But I couldn't do something like 'Mistreated' with Ian Gillan. He wouldn't have done it."

Decades later Ian Paice recalled: "It was meant to be a free-flowing kind of thing. It never got off the ground mainly because Phil wasn't really a good enough bassist yet. He had the voice, but learning to play bass well takes time. And for a thing like that to work, all three players need to be at a certain level. Phil just wasn't there yet."

The name Baby Face would end up being used as a song title on Lizzy's next album, and the Irish band would record a Deep Purple tribute album in 1972 under the name Funky Junction, with vocals provided by Benny White of Irish group Elmer Fudd (see page 75). "Phil was bowled over by Blackmore," Lizzy drummer Brian Downey later said. "That was the first time I'd ever seen him hesitate about anything."

Funky Claude was running in and out

The story behind Deep Purple's time in Montreux and the burning down of the casino during a Frank Zappa and the Mothers of Invention concert is probably the single most documented event in the band's career and the catalyst for their most well known song 'Smoke On The Water'.

The band have been continually asked about, and retold the story endless times throughout the years. But Claude Nobs, the man who was central to the events, has been interviewed far less about it. Shortly before his death in 2013, he told his side of the story to Drew Thompson for Deep Purple (Overseas) Ltd.

As far as Nobs was concerned the original plan was to produce two albums during their time in Switzerland. "Because the live recording they had planned to do was in Montreux at the end of the season it would have been called *Made in Switzerland*, instead of *Made in Japan*! They were still to do the studio album *Machine Head*, but also do a live album which would have been called *Made in Switzerland*, which was a very nice name."

There have been conflicting stories about who was responsible for causing the fire that destroyed the vast complex of which the casino was just one part. Everything from another promoter, to Czech political refugees. A few days after the event Roger Glover told *Melody Maker* that a "gentleman" of Oriental or Asiatic origin let off a distress flare. Nobs recalled: "It was a kid from Czechoslovakia with a flare gun that you would use on a boat. Like Poof! Nothing. But then the ceiling was made with some very flammable things that you would not get away with these days. And then the air-conditioning system started to go crazy because there was more and more heat. The system was designed to get faster in the heat. So, then the fire went into the system... the big wheel. Then everybody went out and it was winter, so with the heat of the ceiling... it went up to the ceiling and the roof was under repair, so there were a lot of windows open. It made a big draught... Poof! In half an hour it was over."

"I was there next to Frank Zappa on stage, and he broke a big window with his guitar, and then he picked up the mic and said very quietly, "There is a fire. Please go out quietly." With big bow windows, with openings to the swimming pool to one side, people didn't have to run, so they just walked outside. Within two minutes, everyone was out and watching the fire. Some people said, "You know, Frank really knows how to finish the show. Now, look what he is doing!"

"We made sure that people got out of the hall; it was done very quickly. Then I went downstairs in the cellar in the kitchen, and I was the last one to leave the casino, and brought out the mother of the manager of the casino. She was the last one in the kitchen, so, I took her by the hand and I said, 'Let's

Mothers lose gear in fire

FRANK ZAPPA and the Mothers lost all their equipment when a raging fire broke out at the Montreux Casino where they were playing a concert on Saturday night.

The fire wrecked the hall, but both the group and the audience — which included Deep Purple — escaped unhurt. The fire occurred midway through Zappa's set.

The Rolling Stones' mobile recording studio was parked outside the Casino during the blaze, but the MM understands this was unaffected by the flames.

Zappa was forced to cancel a concert in Paris on Sunday evening, and he and the group were due to arrive in Britain on Monday. They will hire new equipment in London for their four sell-out concerts at London's Rainbow Theatre on Friday and Saturday.

The group were rehearsing at the Rainbow with the new equipment this week.

Aynsley Dunbar, the Mothers' drummer, said they had completed about an hour and 40 minutes of their set, and were just starting on the solos in "King Kong," when they suddenly noticed people standing up in the hall.

"We saw a glimmer of fire and then a guy appeared with an extinguisher. As the flames began to get higher we made tracks for the exit but Frank said be calm and for everyone in the audience to make for the exits, so we waited while they filed out. Then we ran outside and stood there.

"We thought they had the fire under control, and that it would be nothing, but then someone apparently opened a door. There was a big draught amd smoke swept through. Flames were reaching the top of a 20-storey building next door, because the place was made mostly of wood, with brick only on the outside. When we went back for the gear the casino had all burnt down."

Dunbar estimates that the cost of the equipment lost, which included three synthesisers and an organ, amounted to about £20,000. The Mothers are spending this week looking for new equipment. Aynsley, who lived in London before he joined Zappa, has fared better than the rest of The Mothers. He has got hold of a more or less complete Mayman kit. Luckily, the equipment was insured.

None of The Mothers themselves were injured, although an English road manager, Tony Dodds, was blown out of a window and had to have seven stiches in a finger. According to Dunbar, the finger was "split like a sausage down the middle."

Apart from this incident, the tour has gone very well, apparently, with the band receiving tremendous ovations in Rotterdam.

go out.' And that's it."

Claude immediately put his own problems to one side and focussed on finding Purple an alternative place to record. "We first went to Le Pavilion across from the Montreux Palace and I said to the guys, 'We can record only until 10 in the evening due to the noise carrying across the mountains. We will finish it then and go out for dinner at 10.00.' Of course, the first night they finished at 4.00 in the morning, then they had the police there, so I had to find another place. I found this hotel, The Grand Hotel. Then we had to find a soundproof place at the hotel. We took a gangway In the middle of the hotel, put some absorbing material, about hundred mattresses to get the sound of the drum right. And then we had to go through the balcony, into the toilet and the bathroom, into the studio."

When he was looking for alternative venues various underground bunkers were considered. Something Switzerland has a lot of as he explained. "It's not just in Montreux. There is a law in Switzerland that came out after Hiroshima, I believe, where if you would build a new house, you had to have an atomic shelter with certain dimensions depending on how big the house is, and how many people lived in it... and any big school, commercial centre etc would have to have quite large shelters."

"So, we looked at a big shelters but they were all concrete. They were very cold, very depressing, so I looked for other places. The Montreux Palace was not good enough because it was too loud for the neighbours. With the Grand Hotel we spent a lot of time, and some money to make it completely soundproof to the outside." But the money spent "on a few red lights and a few old beds" was money well spent. Especially as they got the use of the Grand Hotel for free!

The most interesting story that Nobs recalled is one that had a huge impact on Deep Purple's career. "One night, they rang, and came with a Phillips cassette and said, 'We just had a friend do a little thing for you which will not be on the album.' They put the cassette on my player, and it was 'Smoke On The Water'. I said, What? It's incredible!' And they said, 'You think so? We should put it on the album? You don't want to keep it to listen to?' I said, 'Oh, no. It *has* to be on the album!' They gave me that number, I could have kept 'Smoke On The Water' on my own!"

Deep Purple slaps injunction on Richard Branson

It's hard to imagine now but one of Britain's most successful and well-known entrepreneurs was once involved in a legal dispute with Deep Purple. In 1971 Richard Branson was just setting off on his career. He had opened his first record store under the *Virgin* brand name in London's Notting Hill Gate, and soon opened another store in Oxford Street. As well as supplying albums at noticeable discounts compared to the major retail chains of the day, he also took it upon himself to sell imported stock, but he fell foul of the law for allegedly not paying import duties. Other imports were in fact bootlegs: Illegal recordings from the most popular artists of the day such as Crosby, Stills and Nash, Led Zeppelin and Deep Purple.

Of these the Deep Purple album called *H-Bomb* was a live recording of a gig at the Reiterstadion, Aachen, Germany, 10 July 1970. It featured just three tracks, 'Black Night', a cover of the Rolling Stones 'Paint It, Black', and a twenty-minute recording of 'Wring That Neck'. The recording had previously been bootlegged in 1970 as two single albums under the titles *Space Vol 1 & 2*, with the second disc including a thirty-three minute version of 'Mandrake Root' split over two sides but this release had remained relatively underground. Once it was repackaged as a single album (excluding 'Mandrake Root' in the process) it started to receive greater attention and was being sold openly in stores around the country.

Although bootlegs were still a new phenomenon at the time, unlike most others, which were crudely recorded by an audience

M E M O R A N D U M

Date 24th January 1972

From   Christine Seville

Copies to Peter Smits
Tony Edwards

To   Ronnie Beck

Re: "H-BOMB" - Deep Purple
Bootleg L.P.

Mr. Grant of Joynson Hicks telephoned me with the result of our Summary Judgement which was heard on Friday in respect of the sale of the above L.P.

The Court ruled:

1.   A Permanent Injunction against Richard Branston - which means he must not sell or distribute copies of this L.P,

2.   Order for Delivery - this means that Branston must deliver copies of the L.P. which he holds but has not yet sold, and must also deliver plates and/or tapes, etc.

3.   Damages for infringement - these are yet to be assessed by the Master.

4.   Costs - no figures yet.

5.   Order for Discovery - this means that Branston must deliver a list of all documents in his possession relating to this L.P. (where he obtained it, invoices, etc.) within 14 days. Our solicitors then have 7 days in which to inspect them.

Mr. Grant will advise us as soon as the Master has assessed damages and costs.

Re: "DEEP PURPLE DOES IT AGAIN" Vols 1 & 2

Another Summary Judgement against Richard Branston will be heard this Friday in respect of the above L.P.

member with a microphone, either on a cassette or open reel recorder, the sound of this recording was much more professional. Legend has it that the enterprising people behind it had managed to take a direct feed from the stage, and recorded the sound to a stereo recorder concealed in a Volkswagen Camper van. Such was the quality of the recording that it received acknowledgement through the music press, with very few people at the time seemingly concerned about its legal status.

The band members were regularly asked about it in interviews. The ever-ingenious Blackmore cleverly tried to put people off from buying it. The

TELEGRAMS INLAND & OVERSEAS HUMFRIV LONDON W 1   TELEPHONE   01-437 5254-9

B. FELDMAN AND CO. LTD.
MUSIC PUBLISHERS
64 DEAN STREET, LONDON, W1V 6AU

DIRECTORS   J F M DAY   E C DAY   B DAY, F.C.A.   A HOLMES   A C CURRI   R G. MICELI   C A BEUTLINER   D LIVINGSTONE

24th January 1972

CS/RG

Mr. Tony Edwards,
HEC Enterprises Ltd.
25 Newman Street,
London, W.1.

Dear Tony,

Re: Deep Purple Bootlegs

Please find attached details of the outcome of the Summary Judgement against Richard Branston of Virgin Records which was held last Friday. If you have any queries, please give me a ring.

As you will see, another Summary ... heard this Friday, 28th, in respect of DEEP PURPLE ... Grant managed to purchase from Virgin

Hope you had a successful trip

Kindest regards,

27 JAN1972

IN THE HIGH COURT OF JUSTICE   1971.-B.-No.f...

QUEEN'S BENCH DIVISION

The Hon Mr Justice Bristow

B E T W E E N:

B. FELDMAN & COMPANY LIMITED

Plaintiff

- and -

RICHARD CHARLES NICHOLAS BRANSON
(Trading as Virgin Records)

Defendant

Upon hearing Counsel for the Plaintiff and upon reading the Affidavit of Patrick Dennis Frank Grant and upon reading the Summons for Judgment under Order 14 It is ordered that Judgment be entered for the Plaintiff against the Defendants for an injunction restraining them for importing selling or by way of trade exposing or offering for sale any copies of the long-playing record entitled "H.Bomb Deep Purple" and numbered ASC-001

And further for damages for infringement of copyright and for conversion to be assessed and judgment for the delivery up to the Plaintiff of all copies of the said long-playing record with costs to be taxed or agreed.

And it is further ordered that the Defendant do within 14 days serve the Plaintiff with a List of Documents stating what records are or had been in their possession custody or power relating to any question or matter in this cause and file an affidavit verifying such List and that there

end of 'Mandrake Root' on *Space Vol 2* included Blackmore's guitar destruction during the songs' climactic ending. Despite it not appearing on *H-Bomb* he nevertheless claimed that the stage had caught fire and that for twenty minutes of the album all that can be heard is burning wood!

Other members appeared to give it more credence. Roger Glover took it as a compliment, whereas Jon Lord did his best to seemingly increase its sales potential. "Everything was mic'd up to the machine, so they were getting a beautiful sound. I play an amazing organ solo on it, best thing I've heard me doing and miles ahead of my studio stuff, so I reckon we must get into putting down some stage work on tape."

However, the fact remained that it had been recorded and released without the consent of the band or its management, HEC Enterprises. It was something that the latter took exception to and the young Branson was at the brunt of their dissatisfaction. On behalf of HEC Enterprises the band's publisher's B. Feldman & Co. Ltd, filed for a court hearing against Richard Branston, as he was referred to in the correspondence! By January 1972 the courts had ruled that a permanent injunction be imposed on Branson's *Virgin Records*, stopping him from selling or distributing the album. It also insisted he had to return all stock of the said product, whilst damages were also awarded to the claimant. They repeated the procedure for a second Deep Purple bootleg title called *Deep Purple Do It Again Vol 1 & 2*, which was just another version of the same recording.

The fines imposed on Branson looked in danger of derailing his fledgling business venture and his mother had to re-mortgage the family home to help him pay them. However as history has shown, Branson continued to prosper and by 1973 had earned enough money from the record shop to set up his own label and finance its first release, *Tubular Bells* by Mike Oldfield. The unexpected success of that album was the springboard that propelled Branson to the position he holds today as one of Britain's wealthiest people.

Perhaps the most ironic twist in this particular tale is that eight years later, by which time Purple had split, Ian Gillan then pursuing a solo career, signed to *Virgin Records* and had his most successful period outside of Purple, with a string of hit albums and singles for Branson's label.

As for the recording that caused all the controversy, it eventually received an official release, using the original bootleg name of *Space Vol 1 & 2* in 2001 under *Purple Records' Sonic Zoom* imprint, which was set up to release official Deep Purple bootlegs in conjunction with Deep Purple (Overseas) Ltd.

Thin Lizzy -
The first Deep Purple tribute band

Tribute bands are a common part of the music scene in the twenty-first century, and essentially a recent phenomenon. There are now many Purple tribute bands around the world, but as far as Purple tributes are concerned, it all started in 1972 with Funky Junction, which included members of the emerging Thin Lizzy. However unlike tributes of today that generally just perform the songs live, this was the opposite. They merely recorded and released an album called *Funky Junction Play a Tribute to Deep Purple* in January 1973.

The project was the brainchild of German businessman Leo Muller, who contacted Thin Lizzy to record the album. Naturally the band wasn't enthusiastic about it, as they were trying to forge their own style and identity, but the money offered was clearly attractive. Lizzy had just moved to London in order to further their career but as Eric Bell said, "We were virtually starving. To keep the band on the road we needed so much money each week for roadies and the office. Basically this guy spoke with our manager and said he wanted us to record an album of Deep Purple's greatest hits". Despite Phil Lynott being the band's bassist and vocalist, he wasn't comfortable with the idea of tackling Ian Gillan's vocal style, so the band brought in Benny White, singer with another Dublin group Elmer Fudd.

This band generally performed Deep Purple covers during its gigs. Lizzy drummer Brian Downey referred to White as 'really an Ian Gillan clone'. As Lizzy didn't have a keyboard player, Elmer Fudd's Dave Lennox, was also roped in to the project. Thin Lizzy guitarist Eric Bell stated that White and Lennox were each paid "around £60" to travel to De Lane Lea Studios in London to record the album, where ironically some of Deep Purple's recordings had been done.

According to Downey the makeshift band rehearsed for "two or three hours" before recording the whole album in one day. Nine tracks were recorded, with five being Deep Purple songs. Three others were loosely improvised instrumentals all credited to Leo Muller. As Bell explained, the Purple songs were the most well known at that point in time, namely 'Fireball', 'Black Night', 'Strange Kind Of Woman', 'Hush' and 'Speed King' - clearly chosen for maximum commercial impact. The album was released in the UK and the USA on the *Stereo Gold Award* label, and on the *Sonic Records* label in Germany. For the German release, the band's name was changed to The Rock Machine with the album title being changed to *The Rock Machine Play the Best of Deep Purple*.

Thin Lizzy was paid £1000 for the recording although any mention of their name was entirely omitted. The front cover live band shot was actually of Hard Stuff, a *Purple Records* signing band that featured John Gustafson and John Du Cann. The album sleeve declared: *Funky Junction are an exciting new group that has the pulse of today. In this tribute to Deep Purple, they play many of Purple's hits. U.K. and world wide audiences are acclaiming them for the great group they are.* The album bombed. With Purple in full flow at the time, the idea of a band covering its greatest hits wasn't remotely appealing to audiences in 1973.

Ironically the previous year Lynott had already teamed up with Blackmore and Paice for the aborted Baby Face project. Assuming they socialised with Lynott after that, one wonders whether or not the covering of Purple songs was discussed between them or if it was, just what Blackmore and Paice thought of it?

The Loudest Band In The World?
"I'd rather have a five-legged rabbit!"

In 1972 Deep Purple was officially declared the loudest band in the world when it was recorded in the *Guinness Book Of World Records* that they had attained 117 decibels at a concert at the Rainbow Theatre, which purportedly knocked out three members of the audience.

But was that really the case? At a US concert by Led Zeppelin in 1969, The American Speech-Language-Hearing Association apparently recorded a volume of 130dB during the song 'Heartbreaker'. A year later, Daniel Kreps of *Rolling Stone* Magazine wrote that the Led Zeppelin number 'Whole Lotta Love' was the loudest on stage in 1970.

Deep Purple's show at the Rainbow Theatre in London's Finsbury Park on 30 June was the first gig there following a brief four-month period where it closed down in early March. A specially formed company called Biffo, which was run by Chris Wright and Terry Ellis, the bosses of the *Chrysalis* organisation, had acquired the lease on the premises. Artists and groups recording for the *Chrysalis* label, or handled for management or agency by *Chrysalis*, were planned to be among the first attractions featured at the re-born Rainbow, but Purple's two shows on 30 June and 1 July re-opened it.

They were Purple's only UK shows during the summer of '72, having spent March through to early June playing larger venues in the States, followed by an isolated show in Iceland on 19 June and a rare two week break before the Rainbow shows.

PETER BOWYER Presents

DEEP PURPLE

SUPPORTED BY

SILVER HEAD

FRIDAY, 30th JUNE
and
SATURDAY, 1st JULY
both at 7.30 p.m.

TICKETS: £1.50, £1.25, £1.00, 75p

All Tickets available from:
Rainbow Theatre, 232 Seven Sisters Road, London, N.4
Box Office Tel: 01·272 2224 — Tube Station: Finsbury Park

Buses: 19, 29, 106, 259, 298, 168a, 210, 221, 236, 253, 279 W2, W3, W7

The venue had been re-named and was previously called The Astoria, which was clearly still in Ritchie Blackmore's mind when he regaled the story sometime later: "At the end of that tour we played what was then the Astoria at Finsbury Park, with all this stuff, and it was only a three thousand seater! The problem was that once you get used to playing at a certain volume level it's very difficult to back off - it becomes almost like a security blanket - and the thinking was also that if you didn't play at that volume level then you

LOUDEST ROCK GROUP: The amplification for Deep Purple on their 10,-000 watt Marshall P. A. system attains 117 decibels. This was sufficient in the Rainbow Theater, London, in 1972, to render three members of their audience unconscious.

weren't giving of your best. Unknown to us, the *Guinness* people were there - it wasn't pre-arranged or anything - and so as a result of the volume levels at that gig we became 'the loudest band in the world'!'"

"To us it was a hoot, and we had a good laugh over it - I mean we only held the title for a year I think, before The Who took it over - but we seem to have become the band most associated with that. Now, though, we go out of our way not to be too loud!"

So when the next annual edition of the *Guinness Book of World Records* was published it claimed Deep Purple were recognised as "the loudest pop group when in a concert at the London Rainbow Theatre their sound reached 117dB. Three of their audience members were rendered unconscious."

The documenting of audience members being rendered unconscious does seem far-fetched, even for a credible publication such as *The Guinness Book of World Records* and it's more than likely that those three people passed out through heat exhaustion. After all, it was a packed indoor concert in the height of summer.

Shortly after achieving this somewhat dubious accolade Jon Lord told *Disc & Music Echo*, "I always wanted to be in the *Guinness Book of Records* but I think I would have preferred it to have been for something a little more artistic. Maybe I should have grown the biggest marrow or had a rabbit with five legs."

Four years later, The Who were listed as the "record holder", at 126dB, measured at a distance of 32 metres from the speakers at a concert at The Valley (home ground of Charlton Athletic Football Club) on 31 May 1976, and became duly acknowledged as the loudest band in the world. But it didn't stop people from still referring to Purple as the loudest. Something that even Tommy Bolin had to deal with from time to time: "People would come up to me and say 'Hey is it true you hold the *Guinness Book of Records* as being the world's loudest band?' and I'd say 'I don't know. I wasn't even in the band at the time'."

Others have subsequently been officially documented as louder. New

York band Manowar scored *Guinness'* recognition for the loudest musical performance at 129.5 db in 1984. They claim to have reached or exceeded that level again in 1994, but this time the famed book of records refused to acknowledge that accomplishment. *Guinness* has since stopped including a category for world's loudest band, supposedly because of the dangers of hearing damage caused by those hell bent on becoming world record holders.

Because Deep Purple was the first band officially acknowledged as the loudest, despite never really being louder than anyone else, that legacy has continued unabated. The band's own press release in 1993 for *The Battle Rages On* claimed that they still held the title as the loudest band in the world, when it simply wasn't true.

In March 2012, Deep Purple's reputation was brought up in the most unexpected of places. John Bercow, the speaker in the House of Commons in the British Parliament, and the man responsible for keeping order within the chamber, alluded to the band during an interview with Tom Stevenson when the subject of Parliamentary rowdiness was broached. "We wouldn't want to lose all the drama and turn MPs into Trappist monks, but we also need to have serious substantial debate. Planned artificial heckling, especially when it gets to the volume that it sometimes does, which Deep Purple would have been proud of, doesn't add to that."

Made in Japan - Made in England

Deep Purple's seminal double live album recorded in Japan in 1972 is without doubt one of the band's greatest recorded moments. Given Purple's reputation as a live act it seems strange that it took them so long to make such a recording, and it probably would never have happened without the initial suggestion of the Japanese record company who wanted a souvenir of the band's first appearance in the land of the rising sun.

Once they had agreed to the idea they were also adamant if it was going to be recorded that it should be done properly. As such, their trustworthy engineer Martin Birch was employed to record the three shows the band played in Osaka and Tokyo. Once they had heard the playback the band was so taken aback by the quality of the recordings that what was originally planned solely for the Japanese market, got worldwide release as *Made In Japan.*

However *Warner Bros* in Japan elected to do things differently and called the album *Live In Japan.* They also mistakenly credited the recording to just the Tokyo show when in fact it was exactly the same as all other released versions, namely a compilation of the best performances over the three nights.

There was however one notable difference between the Japanese release and those for the rest of the world and that was the cover art. *Warner's* in Japan produced their own cover design which naturally contained photographs from the actual concerts. For the rest of the world *EMI Records* in conjunction with Roger Glover produced a different design all together. Glover's design on the inner spread of the gatefold sleeve utilised the rising sun imagery symbolic with Japan. But when it came to selecting the photographs, *EMI Records* elected not to use photos made in Japan, but instead chose images made in England, by renowned photographer Fin Costello.

To be more precise the front shot was taken at the Rainbow Theatre the band had done a few weeks prior to the Japanese gigs - the shows that earned the band the dubious honour of the loudest band in the world. In fact if you look closely at the bottom right hand side of the front cover you can clearly make out the *Rainbow* logo imprinted on the front of the stage, in between the silhouettes of the front row of the audience. The back cover was shot at another London show at the Brixton Sundown, just over a month after the Japanese gigs on 30th September. The image includes amongst the crowd, none other than Def Leppard guitarist Phil Collen. "I remember getting *Made*

In Japan and looking at that shot on the back and realising it was me – the blond chap standing in the audience right in front of Ritchie Blackmore. I thought, 'that's not Japan! That's Brixton!' It was the first show I'd ever been to, I was 14, and I got right up against the stage. I didn't play guitar yet, and it was that show, standing in front of where Blackmore was on the stage, flashing his *Strat*, playing all this stuff no one else did in those days, that made me pick up a guitar and say 'okay, I want to do that for a living.' I pestered my mum and dad for two years to get me a guitar."

It is unclear why they elected to use photos from English gigs, although getting good photos of Deep Purple at this time was difficult anyway as the band favoured the extensive use of red lights, which any photographer will tell you is their worst possible scenario. It has to be said the Japanese ones used were rather blurry, out of focus shots taken from above and behind the band and probably fell short of *EMI's* standards.

Tour manager Colin Hart puts forward another theory: "The audiences in Japan back then were usually required to remain seated and the front rows were quite far from the high stages. This would make shots of a live show over there look rather dull!"

Although it was released on *Warner Bros* in America, Canada, and Japan, for Europe, through *EMI* it was on the *Purple* label, with the exception of Greece, where Deep Purple's records continued to be released on the *Harvest* label.

None of this should detract from the finished product though. With no overdubs of any kind, when it was released, *Made In Japan* served as the finest advert imaginable for Deep Purple's phenomenal live performances. In fact, stuff your loudest band in the world tag. Most fans would settle for most exciting live band in the world! Yep, don't think many bands could compete with Purple's power, virtuosity and sheer excitement.

Even though the various band line-ups have gone on to release many other live albums over the years, *Made In Japan* is still the favourite for the vast majority of fans, even though the cover was made in England!

At Last... Deep Purple's music for group & orchestra

It has often been cited that Jon Lord's *Concerto For Group & Orchestra* pioneered the way for future collaborations by other artists. To a degree this may well be the case, but the likes of Keith Emerson was also doing such things at the time with The Nice (see page 35), and The Moody Blues had also released their *Days of Future Passed* album, complete with orchestra, almost two years earlier. Certainly Lord's "Concerto" was the first real effort of combining the two musical genres in such a specific way, although pop records from the fifties onwards had used orchestration.

Lord's approach was certainly different, and although tracks such as 'Anthem' and 'April' on Purple's second and third albums respectively also incorporated orchestral arrangements, there was never a concerted effort to arrange Deep Purple's own songs for group & orchestra.

Step forward James Last. Born Hans Last, 17 April 1929, the German composer and big-band arranger established the James Last Orchestra in 1964 - a big-band orchestra with strings. In 1965 Last released an album, *Non-Stop Dancing*, a recording of brief renditions of popular songs, all tied together by an insistent dance beat and crowd noises. It was such a success that it helped make him a major European star. Over the next four decades, astonishingly Last released over 190 records, including several more volumes of *Non-Stop Dancing*. Any of the popular tunes of the day were deemed worthy of the Last treatment and between 1970-73 he transformed five Purple tunes with his orchestra.

'Fireball' (from the 1972 LP *Non Stop Dancing 1972 – 2*, Polydor 2371 269) has to be the pick of the bunch for it's sheer madness. Last's interpretation of this thunderous, hard riffing song defies description, but if you can imagine a typical James Last style complete with a backing chorus chanting the melody you get some idea as to how far removed this is from the original. Truly astonishing! The same album includes 'Never Before', with both tracks credited as being composed by Blackmore, Lillian, Clover, Lord & Paice. Three out of five ain't bad I suppose!

The songs were often woven into medleys with other tunes of the day. For example on *Non Stop Dancing 12* (Polydor 2371-141) 'Strange Kind of Woman' was the third part of a medley with The Ronettes 'Be My Baby' and Led Zeppelin's 'The Immigrant Song'. Once again the composer credit is incorrect, as only Lord and Gillan are listed as the writers. Even more ironic, given Blackmore's comments on the song (see page 62).

For the record the other two songs Last's Orchestra did were 'Black Night' on the 1970 LP *Non Stop Dancing 11* (Polydor 2371 111), and the final one to get the Last make-over was 'Woman From Tokyo' on the 1973 release, *Non Stop Dancing 1973 - 2* (Polydor 2371 376). Although catalogue numbers for each of the albums have been included here I don't suspect too many Purple fans are likely to be rushing out to add these to their collections. But with the volumes of sales Last has achieved, the composer royalties would have been a nice boost to the band's income. I just wonder what happened to Blackmore, Paice and Glover's share for 'Strange Kind of Woman' and whether or not a separate account was created for Lillian!

In 1992 Cromwell Productions decided to go the full hog and orchestrate a full album of Purple classics. They commissioned the Moscow Symphony Orchestra and recorded and released *A Symphonic Tribute To Deep Purple* (Cromwell CPCD 018) containing interpretations of 'Smoke On The Water', 'Highway Star', 'Fireball', 'Lazy, 'Burn', 'Space Truckin',' 'The Mule', 'Child in Time' and 'Pictures Of Home'. Rumours abound at the time that Blackmore had been approached to play over the orchestrations and that they had arranged flights, hotel and travel, only for him to send a two-line fax just two days before the recording, saying that he decided to pass up the offer.

Four years later Purple took the first step at re-arranging their songs for additional instruments with a brass section augmenting some numbers on stage at a gig in Paris. These were captured on the album *Live At The Olympia '96*. They took it a step further in 1999 as part of the 30th anniversary shows for *Concerto For Group & Orchestra* with Jon Lord orchestrating some Purple songs for the event to be performed with the London Symphony Orchestra and subsequently released on *Live At The Royal Albert Hall*. The following year they rolled it out for a full-scale tour, and have done further tours since with orchestral backings. In 2011 they toured America and Europe with a 38-piece Orchestra augmenting Purple music that was billed as "The Songs That Built Rock". Two DVDs from the tour, of consecutive night's performances have been released - *Live In Montreux 2011* and *Live In Verona*.

Fittingly the band performed a seven-song set with the Orion Orchestra at the *Celebrating Jon Lord* concert at the Royal Albert Hall in 2014. These included new orchestrations for 'Uncommon Man' and 'Above And Beyond' from the *NOW What?!* album, and Lord's own orchestration for 'Perfect Strangers'. It was the first time the band had performed the *NOW What?!* songs with an orchestra.

That it took Purple so long to orchestrate some of their songs is somewhat surprising given the classical undertones to much of the music. A case of last but certainly not least.

Did the Bay City Rollers really help Purple get their new vocalist?

David Coverdale's appointment as lead singer in August 1973 is a true fairytale story of epic proportions. Following Ian Gillan's departure, Blackmore had his heart set on arguably the finest vocalist of the era, namely Paul Rodgers of Free. Free had just split for the second and final time, but Rodgers was not convinced, particularly when the music press reported that he would be joining the band in advance of any firm decision. He duly opted to get a new band together, which became Bad Company.

Although in theory, with Purple at the peak of its popularity, the band could have sought any one of a number of high profile vocalists, but astonishingly they also considered amateurs and semi-pros. Step forward David Coverdale who was then playing in the semi-pro band The Fabulosa Brothers in North East England. The band had drawn interest from *Bell Records* and produced an audition tape in 1973 for the label, recorded at Strawberry Studios in Stockport. In a 2011 special Whitesnake edition of *Classic Rock* magazine, the band's guitarist Alan Fearnley recalled: "*Bell* came to see us. Apparently the choice was between either the Fabulosa Brothers or the Bay City Rollers. The Rollers got the deal!"

As fanciful as Fearnley's scenario is, the thought of *Bell Records* signing the Fabulosa Brothers instead, and changing the course of history, with Coverdale possibly not even considering applying for the Purple vacancy, isn't the truth. The Bay City Rollers had been signed to *Bell* for two years prior to The Fabulosa Brothers recording session, and had already released two singles on the label.

However Coverdale's previous band The Government had also made a demo tape in early 1971 at Multicord Studios in Sunderland and it is feasible that this was sent to *Bell Records* but as Fearnley wasn't in The Government, it's unclear whether or not it was this tape that he meant. It's worth mentioning that The Government's booking agent was Barry Perkins who became The Bay City Rollers business manager so there is some connection to all this, even though Fearnley's memory is somewhat awry.

And although *Bell* rejected The Fabulosa Brothers, which temporarily put the young Coverdale's chances of becoming a full-time professional musician on hold, it wasn't for long. Despite crossing paths four years earlier, none of Purple appeared to have remembered Coverdale as they resorted to advertising in the music press for Ian Gillan's replacement. "I was reading the papers and I saw that Purple were still looking for a vocalist. I didn't think about it, every week somebody's looking for a musician. The chick who worked at the boutique I was at was a Purple nut. I remember playing on the bill to them a few years before just after the second chapter of the band. I remember being complimented a lot by Ritchie, Jon and Roger."

"The chick at the boutique took out a copy of *Machine Head* and put it on. Half a dozen guys came into the shop, one of them came up to me and said 'are you still singing', like you'd say 'are you still brushing your teeth', or something like that. I said 'Yeah' and he asked ' why don't you go for a job with Purple' and laughed. I got really depressed and then I really got violent and thought 'I don't want to be regarded as a joke', it means a lot to me.' And then I remembered I knew this chick who knew Purple and I tried to get in contact with them."

However this approach failed and Coverdale's next move was to contact some of the influential friends he'd made when he supported bands in Redcar - and get them to put in a good word with Purple for him but that didn't work either.

"Then I got a friend of mine, Roger Barker, who used to be manager of the Redcar Jazz Club, to take over for me, I rang him up and I said: 'I'm going after the job with Purple' and there was a deadly silence. Everyone I told had faith in me but that was like aiming my sights a little too high. I think they thought I should have started a little lower down the scale."

But Coverdale soon found himself auditioning for Purple at Scorpio Sound Studios in London. Just over a year after the event, Coverdale told Pete Makowski in an interview for *Sounds*, "We did a couple of old rock things which was embarrassing because I didn't know the words, I wasn't around at the time. I learnt 'Smoke On The Water' and 'Strange Kind Of Woman' and they didn't play either of those." Decades later Coverdale told the story that he did do 'Strange Kind Of Woman' at his audition and that Blackmore told him, the way he sung it was the way he had originally envisaged it, but his memory from 1974 was probably more accurate!

So having been rejected by *Bell Records*, and in doing so, denying Coverdale the chance to be on the same label as the Bay City Rollers, a contract with *Purple Records* became the order of the day. "Sha La La La, Shang-A-Lang" as a certain Scottish band might have said!

Some Kind Of Mystery

Mid-August 1973 and having auditioned David Coverdale at Scorpio Sound Studios in London, Blackmore, Lord, Paice and bassist Glenn Hughes, who had been recruited the previous month all agreed that Coverdale was the lead vocalist needed to complete the new line-up. The news was not announced until a month later.

Meanwhile, with Coverdale presumably back up north celebrating his new job as lead singer of the biggest selling album artists in America, Hughes, Lord and Paice had their first recording session together on Saturday, 1st September at Studio A of Lansdowne Recording Studios in London's Holland Park area. The very place where legendary independent producer Joe Meek worked in the early part of his career.

It is not clear exactly how much was recorded, but two tracks still exist; a John Ellison composition that had been a minor US hit in 1967 for the Soul Brothers Six, called 'Some Kind Of Wonderful', and another track titled 'Don't Know Yet'. The fact that both are listed in the Deep Purple (Overseas) Ltd archives as first takes, does suggest there was more than one run through of each, but this cannot be confirmed.

Both tracks are quite funky and nothing remotely like the material recorded two months later for the *Burn* album. With Blackmore also not present, Hughes added lead guitar work to 'Some Kind Of Wonderful' as well as backing vocals, on a song that he most likely suggested for the session. 'Don't Know Yet' is an instrumental jam and very reminiscent of the material that Paice and Lord would produce three years later with Paice Ashton Lord. Ian Paice produced the session, which was engineered on 16-track by Ashley Howe.

It's unlikely that the Ellison song was ever considered for *Burn*, but the following year it was recorded by Grand Funk Railroad and released on their album *All the Girls in the World Beware!!!* In an article published in the American *Guitar Player* magazine the month before the Lansdowne session Blackmore was asked, "Why do you suppose groups like Grand Funk are selling millions of records when there are other bands that are doing the same thing only much better?"

"America is so vast," Blackmore replied, "that I think people buy records mainly of groups they've seen, and I imagine that since they must have seen Grand Funk all over America, they buy their records. At the same time I have not met one person who likes Grand Funk."

Despite his dislike for Grand Funk, 'Some Kind Of Wonderful' was a number 3 US hit in 1975. Blackmore would undoubtedly have heard it on American radio at the time but the question remains: did he ever hear the Lord, Paice and Hughes' version and what was the session intended for? Now that's some kind of mystery!

Music in my head
or better left unsaid?

Around the time that Deep Purple with David Coverdale was touring the States promoting *Burn*, former lead singer Ian Gillan was busy at work in his recently acquired De Lane Lea recording studios, which he had renamed Kingsway. Free from the structure of Purple, Gillan started working on his debut album, incorporating styles that were far removed from his former band. With Gillan still signed to Purple's management the plan was to release the album on *Purple Records*.

Apart from Purple the label had released many albums and singles since 1971, from an array of different acts. Some, such as Hard Stuff and Silverhead were straight forward rock acts. Other artists included Rupert Hine, whose folk-rock offering *Pick up a Bone* was produced by Roger Glover, and Hawaiian singer Yvonne Elliman, who had appeared on the original *Jesus Christ Superstar* album alongside Gillan. But the label had also released a few oddities such as a single 'Who is the Doctor' by veteran actor Jon Pertwee, then the title character of the BBC sci-fi drama *Doctor Who*. They even produced an album that depicted the story of Colditz, with words and songs from artists including Gracie Fields, Arthur Askey and George Formby.

With that in mind, the songs that Ian Gillan recorded were not particularly extreme. Some tracks such as the covers of 'Ain't That Loving You Baby' and the Elvis Presley number 'Trying To Get To You' were a nod to his rock 'n' roll upbringing. Of the self-penned tracks 'You Make Me Feel So Good' was the most similar to Purple's style. But of the other songs recorded, they veered from the country-rockabilly of 'She Called Me Softly' to ballads with string accompaniment such as 'Music In My Head'.

Gillan had put a lot in to the album and two different versions of most

PURPLE RECORDS
℗ the open ear.

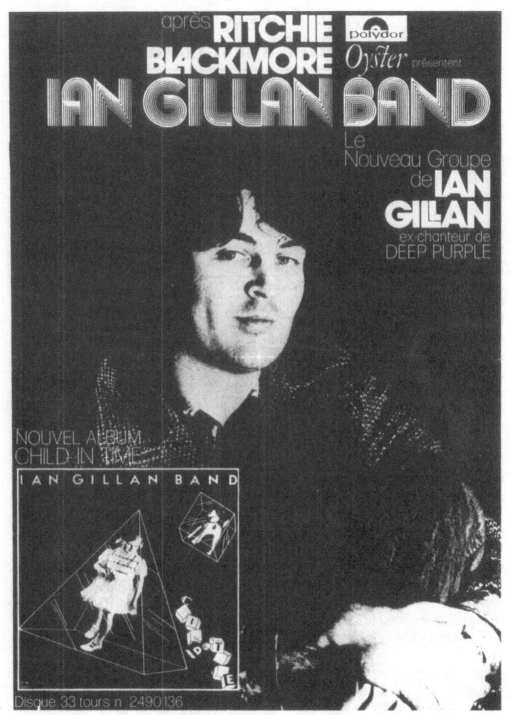

French press advert for Ian Gillan's "first" solo album.
Purple Records could have placed adverts two years earlier for 'Music In My Head'
but thought that it was too diverse for Deep Purple fans.

of the songs were recorded. But *The Open Ear* slogan that *Purple Records* had previously championed didn't apply to Gillan. As he explained several years later, "It's since been referred to as the aborted album, none of the songs of which have seen the light of day. I just play it at home to my friends. I like it, it's one of my favourite albums. But I took it into the office and they said, 'Oh no, this is no good. The public won't like this it's too diversified. It's not what they expect'." Edwards and Coletta felt the material was too radical and refused to release it. Gillan had to lick his wounds. Since leaving Purple he had invested several hundred thousand in to a hotel venture and a motorcycle business and he didn't have sufficient capital to either buy his way out of his contract with the Purple organisation or finance the release of the album.

More than a year passed before he eventually went back in to the studio and re-evaluated his approach, largely down to the Purple management's direction. "They sent me in to a studio and the result was *Child in Time*. They wanted the continuity with Deep Purple. A spin-off on that to start a new career." This time it was with the help of Roger Glover who produced what became the *Child in Time* album by the Ian Gillan Band. 'You Make Me Feel So Good' was re-recorded alongside new songs and a re-arrangement of the Purple classic that gave the album its title added a greater degree of commerciality in to the bargain.

By the time of its release Deep Purple (Overseas) Ltd had set up a subsidiary label, *Oyster Records* to handle Ritchie Blackmore's Rainbow, and the other members solo output. *Child in Time* was also released on *Oyster*, which soon followed with albums by Paice Ashton Lord, and in certain European territories, for David Coverdale.

As the decades rolled on Gillan appeared to distance himself from the recordings and in 1990 he said, "It's just a collection of demos. There's some good songs on there, but it's very private." He clearly had a change of heart because only two years later the unreleased album eventually saw the light of day when it was released along with the tracks from the *Cherkazoo* project (see page 58).

At long last fans could hear the music and make their own decision as to whether or not Deep Purple (Overseas) Ltd had made the right decision eighteen years earlier. A listen to the variety of albums Gillan has released under his own name since, certainly indicate that his willingness to do exactly what he wants certainly wasn't diminished by his initial set back.

Sent to Coventry
with flour power!

Deep Purple MKIII's one and only 25-date UK tour in April and May 1974 saw the band playing many smaller venues despite the band's increasing success. Having just completed the first US tour, where they played to huge audiences, most notably at the all-day California Jam in front of several hundred thousand, the UK leg was a world of difference. Venues such as Norwich Theatre Royal were only ever played on this tour. They even elected to play at three different London venues instead of the logistically easier choice of Earl's Court, where other top acts of the day such as Slade and David Bowie had played the previous year; or even Wembley Empire Pool, which had hosted gigs since the early sixties.

Aside from a re-arranged gig for Southend at the end of June, the tour concluded with two nights at Coventry Theatre on 28th and 29th May. The support act was the American band Elf, featuring Ronnie James Dio who by then were signed to Purple's own label, bonding them closer to the Purple organisation in the process. They had been supporting Purple in America since 1972, so it came as no surprise that *Purple Records* took the opportunity to promote their protégés to British audiences as well.

On the last night in Coventry a degree of end of tour road fever got the better of everyone, as Elf's roadie Raymond D'addario recalls, "We used to play all these little theatres with orchestra pits and one of the last shows we did, Ritchie had the crew go out and get all these bags of flour and they put holes in them and pelted Elf with them. There was Ronnie trying to sing and these little bags of flour hit him and exploded. That was the first time I'd ever seen him do anything like that."

But that wasn't the end of the tale, as the roadies and Elf got their revenge by doing pretty much the same to Purple who were bombarded with flour as 'Space Truckin'' reached its climactic ending. The tomfoolery became even more absurd during the encore. For this tour Purple surprised many fans by closing the show with a blues standard 'Goin' Down', written by Don Nix and originally released by the band Moloch on their eponymous 1969 album. Nix released a version of the song on a single in 1972. The Who, Freddie King, Jeff Beck, and the US band Energy that included Tommy Bolin were amongst the many acts that also covered it.

As Purple played 'Goin' Down' a line of trouserless roadies decided to have a knees up across the stage and to conclude the evening's absurdities a man described as "the Entertainments Manager", who was actually Blackmore's assistant, Ian Broad, strode across the stage in black tights, knee length boots and a hat, looking every inch like a Max Wall impersonator, before baring his buttocks to all and sundry!

If the baring of human flesh bemused fans, more of the same occurred at the rearranged Southend gig that followed on 27th June. A female audience member got up on stage during the second number 'Might Just Take Your Life' and danced topless behind Ian Paice. She returned as the band performed the encore, this time completely naked and dancing around Ritchie Blackmore. Whether or not her antics had any affect on Jon Lord is unclear, but during the show when he was introducing Coverdale and Hughes, he commented that if the Netherlands did not win the FIFA World Cup, he would streak across the stage! The Dutch did in fact lose the final to host nation West Germany on 7th July, but no evidence has come to light that like the naked dancer ten days earlier, Lord ever appeared on stage naked!

COMING ATTRACTIONS AT

Southend
The Kursal Ballroom

THURS. JUNE 27th.

DEEP PURPLE

SAT. JULY 6th.

☆ **SPARKS** ☆

SAT. JULY 13th.

COCKNEY REBEL

Dirty Deeds Done Dirt Cheap

As 1975 began it was business as normal for Purple, and although *Stormbringer* turned out to be less successful than the previous few albums, the band was still hugely popular and couldn't resist the lucrative offer of flying to Australia for a one-off show headlining the Sunbury Festival, held on a farm just north of Melbourne. The gig is best remembered for the way in which the show over ran and Deep Purple's set finished forty minutes later than scheduled.

Whilst this is quite a common occurrence at festival gigs, there were accusations from some quarters that Deep Purple had done this deliberately, because although they were the headlining act, it had been agreed that local band AC/DC would conclude the day's entertainment after Purple's set had finished. Because of the overrun, AC/DC didn't get to perform and a feud started between the two camps that continued for sometime. It might explain Blackmore's comments some time later when he proclaimed AC/DC to be "an all time low in rock 'n' roll." "I like them as friends but I don't like their music," he said on his return to Australia the following year after Sunbury.

In more recent times the memories of what happened have been somewhat distorted. When speaking for VH-1's *Behind The Music* documentary in 2013 Ian Paice said, "AC/DC were the up and coming big Aussie band, and they were on before us, and having a great time, and they played really great, they wouldn't stop. And we had a real tight time schedule to get on, get off before the curfew, get to the airport and get back to Los Angeles. So our tour manager just pulled the plug on them, 'cos they were just having a great time. I mean it happens, you know. But we had to pull the plug on them, which didn't go down very well, as you can imagine. But we had to do our set. Every minute they were on stage was 1 minute less that we could play, 'cos of the curfew. Had we gone up to I think it was 11 o'clock or something, then they'd have pulled the plugs on us. So it was just one of those things. We didn't do it, we didn't tell anybody to do it. But the road manager said, that's it you're finished. He just unplugged them, and that was that."

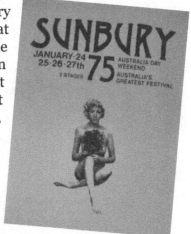

David Coverdale has also commented about this gig in recent years, "Apparently, a young Aussie band had jumped onstage, plugged into our gear and started playing! Well, all hell broke loose, from what I was told. Our roadies (big buggers to a man) wrestled with the young band to get them off our equipment and off the stage. Chaos and frolics ensued."

That Purple caused grief to AC/DC is not in dispute although it certainly did not happen the way Paice described it. In his book *Hell Ain't A Bad Place To Be*, Mick Wall talks of George Young formerly of The Easybeats who had been filling in for AC/DC on bass, getting into a fistfight with Purple. With roadies of either side involved in a scrap, before AC/DC eventually left the stage, refusing to play at all. One report that focused on the New Zealand band The La De Das, who were also on the bill said *The La De Das' appearance was one of the few high points in this ill-fated event, which was marred by bad weather and poor attendance. Headliners Deep Purple copped strong criticism for the arrogant and aggressive conduct of their crew, with Purple's roadies provoking a fight with AC/DC and George Young after refusing to allow AC/DC to follow them on stage. There was also a lot of anger over their whopping AU$60,000 fee - about ten times the going rate for a top-rank Aussie act of the day. Despite these altercations, the La De Das made a positive impression on Deep Purple, and lead guitarist Ritchie Blackmore expressed an interest in jamming with them.*

Almost eleven months later and Australia's top music people are finally to see part compensation for their involvement in this year's washed out Sunbury Rock Festival.
Until now, Australian acts appearing during the festival had not been paid by the liquidated promoters or received compensation from any other source.
Deep Purple, the overseas guests, however, were.
And it is Deep Purple who have had to dig into their pockets to make some reimbursement for the lack of payment to the Australian artistes, at the Musicians' Union's insistence.
Federal spokesman of the Union, Mr Don Cushion, told JUKE: "Under the department of Labour and Immigration laws, any person or persons who is feared might cause industrial unrest may be refused permission to enter the country.
"We made it quite clear to the Minister for Labour and Immigration that the proposed tour of Deep Purple could lead to considerable unrest. Our thoughts were also expressed to the group and they were very understanding.
"Deep Purple as musicians appreciated that our musicians had been disadvantaged and at the time they thought the court would have seen to their interests. There was no hesitation in handing over the money to our trustees."

JUKE understands that there was an undertaking that unless the money was paid to the Union in advance, the tour would undoubtedly have been cancelled.
Earlier this year the equity court ruled that the musicians were to be paid the sum of 1c in every dollar - providing that they could prove they were employers of the festival promoter, Mr John Fowler. Under Victorian law, however, it was proven that the musicians are self-employed at Sunbury and therefore not entitled to any payment from that source.
The Musicians Union say they spent thousands of dollars working on the case, but virtually lost.
"An amount of money was received from Deep Purple and has since been paid into a trust account," says Mr Cushion.
"The money will be paid to the members direct without the union or agencies etc. ever seeing it."
Each musician who appeared at Sunbury will be paid the full musician's rate - the minimum legal entitlement.
The outcome of negotiations has been the fruition of a joint union exercise - A.T.E.A. and The Musician Union.

— FRANK PETERS

Kevin Borich the guitarist with the La De Das said, "If I remember correctly - the Festival was on a Saturday - I'd played my show, then another band played before Purple. I was looking around back stage and came across a caravan with a lot of Strats in it with Ritchie's roadie tuning them up. I said hi and we had a chat. He asked who was the band on before. I said it was me and my band. He said Ritchie liked it and asked if we were playing on Sunday night in Melbourne. I said yeah!. Tell Ritchie to come down and have a blow, thinking he'd never show. Anyhow, we were playing the once-famous Hard Rock Cafe in Melbourne, and it was a night to remember. We were on stage and this roadie comes up with a *Stratocaster* and says 'Uh, Ritchie wants to have a blow' and I said 'Oh!' So all the people pushed to the front of the stage to watch his lightning fingers. We played a song I wrote called 'Celebration' which has an extended second half which is great for jamin' and Ritchie was fantastic - it went on for a long time and was the highlight of the night. We had a good play and a bit of a drink and talk after. He enjoyed the blow, most polite of him to come down because I don't think he's the kind of guy who fucks around."

Back to Sunbury and AC/DC weren't the only band to suffer at the hands of Purple. With the promoters, Odessa Promotions guaranteeing Purple AU$60,000, the knock on affect was an increase in ticket prices. The previous year the full 3-day ticket cost AU$12, with Queen headlining, but for Purple they had hiked the price up to AU$20. Allied to the unusually poor weather that reduced the site to a mud bath, only 16,000 tickets were sold compared to 30,000 the previous year.

After paying Deep Purple, Odessa Promotions was liquidated, which meant the other acts did not get paid, with the exception of one who had arranged for sponsorship from independent sources. Unpaid staff and performers lodged a string of lawsuits against Odessa Promotions. Although the equity court ruled that the Australian artists weren't entitled to Odessa's assets, as they were self-employed individuals rather than employees of Odessa Promotions, the Musicians Union won a small victory for the artists in question. As part of the conditions for Deep Purple touring Australia, the band had paid a portion of their fee to the union due to concerns that their presence might cause industrial unrest. The deposit was paid out to Musicians Union members, giving them the minimum rate at that time. Had this not happened Purple may well have not been able to return to Australia, which they did later in the year with new guitarist Tommy Bolin.

Tasting Deep Purple
behind the Iron Curtain

During Purple's most commercially successful period in the mid seventies, a large area of Europe was pretty much out of bounds - the countries of Central and Eastern Europe that had fallen under Communist control after the Second World War. The Communist states did much in their power to ensure their citizens were not exposed to Western influence, and this included the pop and rock music, that largely hailed from Britain and America. In some countries heavy fines were often imposed upon people found in possession of illegally imported records from what they saw as the decadent West. Despite this, records did manage to reach some of the youth and were shared discreetly amongst many. 'Child in Time' was one such song that became an anthem for Deep Purple fans behind the Iron Curtain.

Ian Gillan: "As far as the Eastern Bloc is concerned, or behind the Iron Curtain as it was known, our music was forbidden. I've spoken to many people who learned their English from forbidden albums by bands like Deep Purple. They understood what 'Child in Time' was about (the Cold War) and that there were kids on the other side of the Berlin Wall who felt the same as they did. I met a guy who did three years in gaol for possession of *Deep Purple In Rock* — personally speaking I thought he should have got a little longer myself (laughter). He jumped up on stage and gave me such a hug he nearly killed me. Three years in gaol is a long time for having a record. So you realise how oppressive it was."

There were a few exceptions however. In 1971 Yugoslavia's state owned label *Jugoton* started releasing Purple records, licensed from *EMI*. From that time on, all the albums from *In Rock* were released in Yugoslavia. The Yugoslavs

more liberal approach also resulted in Purple being the first Western band to perform concerts there when in '75 they kicked off the European tour with two shows on 16 March at the Pioneer Hall, Belgrade, and the following night at the Sportshalle in Zagreb.

But other parts of

OCHUTNÃVKA *DEEP PURPLE*

Eastern Europe were less fortunate. Czechoslovakia did release *Come Taste The Band* (in 1977) on the State run *Supraphon* label, which they re-titled *Ochutnávka Deep Purple*. Translated it simply means *Tasting Deep Purple*. The album came in a unique sleeve, and also included a rather nondescript poster. In 1986 *Supraphon* also released *Perfect Strangers*.

Following the band's split in '76, one of the more oppressive communist countries East Germany, finally released a compilation of Deep Purple recordings the following year on the *Amiga* label. *Amiga* was the pop subsidiary of Deutsche Schallplatten Berlin, the only official record company in what they loved to call the German Democratic Republic! The album consisted of eight tracks from the period 1970-74 with sleeve notes by H.P Hofmann, that well-known Communist Deep Purple authority!

So full of propaganda were they, and to some extent so ludicrously hilarious as a result, they are worth reproducing: *LPs from the years 1970 to 74, from which a compilation was done for this LP, support the idea that the band has the concept of varied rock music yet with their undeniably own sound. As also the compilation you hold in your hands suggests, many Deep Purple recordings show the effort to present situations, thoughts and feelings from real-life situations. That alone keeps them apart from the mass productions by the capitalist music industry, in which lies about idylls and make-believe worlds dominate, supposedly to keep the working people from thinking about their crisis-ridden everyday-life: in the final analysis Lady Double Dealer turns itself against any form of double standards. Speed King is an indirect invitation to live life to the fullest - however whether parties are a necessity to save your soul is a matter of opinion. Rat Bat Blue describes love that in effect is not love. Woman from Tokyo shows the stimulating influence that a beautiful exotic female can have on a young man. Problems are underlying Anyone's Daughter which young people are still confronted with in capitalism, if they dare to marry against their place in society. The irony of the last lines cannot be missed: how about that, after all I've got a rich man's daughter. Hold On includes the candid thoughts of a young man about the subject matter love. In the end it is the quality of the chosen titles, the style of musicianship and the varied sound that explains why the musicians in Deep Purple belong to the most successful and longest-serving in England, who still appear live nowadays. In the age of electronically mixed studio sounds that also speaks for them.*

So now you know what Deep Purple's songs are really all about!

Owed to DP O

Deep Purple fans are divided on the decision to carry on with Tommy Bolin following Blackmore's departure. Whilst it became apparent once the band went on tour that Bolin had a severe drug habit, hindsight is a wonderful thing and initially the band thought it was the right decision. The merits of the music produced also splits fans: *Come Taste The Band* was a vastly different album to any previous Purple LP and with Bolin's style the live shows were a world apart from those with Blackmore at the helm.

But one thing that very few people are aware of is that the organisation was considering dispensing with Bolin even before the band finally called it a day. But the reasoning had nothing to do with the music. It centred on problems with songwriting publishing. When Bolin joined the band he signed contracts in June '75 that should have given him the same deal on publishing as the other band members, but friction arose between Deep Purple (Overseas) Ltd and Bolin, along with his manager Barry Frey.

A problem had arisen through his US publisher that resulted in Bolin having a benefit not extended to the other band members. By January '76 Deep Purple (Overseas) Ltd were of the opinion that Bolin and Frey would never agree to sign paperwork that would address the situation and there were discussions within the organisation as to how best deal with it. Consideration was made as to whether or not the band would be better off with or without their American guitarist.

Even after the band had affectively ceased, following the show at Liverpool's Empire Theatre on 15 March, discussions continued between Deep Purple (Overseas) Ltd and Bolin's lawyers who were acting on behalf of his own publishing company.

Deep Purple (Overseas) Ltd stressed the point that had they been aware of the situation they would never have allowed him to write what he did for the band prior to establishing an agreement with Bolin's publishers. They also stated that if Bolin's publishers had at the time of recording *Come Taste The Band*, adopted the stance they had by then taken, that the band would not have recorded the songs for which he was the main contributor. One wonders, just what that album would have been like, had that situation arose.

As it so happened, Deep Purple had called it a day and it ensured that there would not be another album with Bolin, although the publishing ramifications still had to be addressed as the organisation continued to operate on a business level, despite Deep Purple being defunct.

Did Blackmore Ever See
Deep Purple With Tommy Bolin?

"Ritchie has come and listened to the band
and he really likes it a lot, which makes me happy."
Tommy Bolin

This comment by Tommy Bolin was made during a radio interview in Melbourne on 26 November 1975. The MKIV line-up had barely got out of the starting blocks at the time having only done seven concerts on what would turn out to be its one and only world tour.

Bolin's comment could have been interpreted as implying that Blackmore had caught one of the gigs but with his own band Rainbow in the middle of its own inaugural tour in the States, that was simply not possible. But Blackmore had checked out the new Purple prior to the said tour. Whilst auditioning musicians for Rainbow in June '75 at the large Pirate Sound rehearsal stage in Los Angeles he soon discovered that his fellow band mates were also due at the same place.

Colin Hart who had been Purple's tour manager and who left alongside Blackmore following the latter's last Purple gig in Paris in April '75 documented in his autobiography *A Hart Life*: *One day, noticing that a large amount of equipment was being shipped to the stage next to ours, I, inquisitively as ever, asked who it was. 'Deep Purple for four to five days' came the amused reply. 'They start rehearsals next week'. I told Ritchie who also saw the irony and ordered a week off to avoid any embarrassment to anybody, despite him still having to pay a daily rental to the studios. Nevertheless, Ritchie asked me to 'drop in' to spy on their rehearsals and report back, which I dutifully did. Bolin was good, very good and fitted into the jazz funk direction that Glenn and David were determined to follow. Ritchie's curiosity could not be contained and I drove him down to the studios one afternoon. We quietly entered our sound stage and like two sneak thieves stealthily cracked open the double doors leading to Purple's stage. They were in full flow. Ritchie's face showed no emotion and he listened there for nearly half an hour.*

Eight months later, having completed recording in Germany of his second Rainbow album, *Rising* in February 1976, Blackmore and his band returned to its Los Angeles base. On 27th February Deep Purple was coming to the end of its US tour with a performance at the Long Beach Arena. According to Rainbow keyboard player Tony Carey, when the author interviewed him in 2005, Blackmore asked his band if they wanted to see the gig. "We went with Ritchie to see Deep Purple in Los Angeles. We sat in the tenth row and watched the band with Tommy Bolin. There was no problem. We all sat there in a row like school kids."

In recent times both Blackmore and Colin Hart have said they don't recall seeing Purple MKIV in concert, but the author quizzed Carey again for this book. "We all went from a rehearsal at Pirate Sound to Long Beach Arena to see DP. We sat with crossed-and-critical-arms... and I'm just about completely certain Wally was with us. The band was chaotic, Glenn and Tommy were on 4" platforms and doing a very silly prancy thing... Glenn was screaming a lot - David was fantastic, I was always a huge Coverdale fan, and the best rhythm section / organist in rock kept things in line. The crowd was sort of apathetic; though it looked pretty full... maybe 12,000 at a guess. Tommy was clearly very ill, Glenn not much better, it was (in retrospect) sad I suppose, but I was 22 and not that critical, not to mention my own chemical romance in those days. If Colin remembers it differently, I'll defer to his recollection, but I remember being sort of shocked that RB would even go to the show... he might have been just gloating, or he might have been genuinely curious."

Decades later it's very easy for the memory to play tricks, but when Blackmore was interviewed in Australia on 21 November 1976 for 3DB Radio, he told the interviewer he had seen Purple on stage with Bolin, and a contemporary press review also placed him and Hart backstage at the show.

Although many of Purple's shows on this tour were erratic due to the drug intoxication of both Bolin and Hughes, this particular performance was arguably one of the best. It was also recorded and broadcasted on the *King Biscuit Flower Hour* radio show. This initially produced the bizarrely named bootleg release *On The Wings Of A Russian Foxbat*. The show was officially released in Europe in 1995 under the same title, and in the States as *In Concert*. It was reissued in 2009 as *Live At Long Beach*.

So even though Blackmore and Hart have claimed in recent times that they didn't go, Carey is adamant they did, and the weight of evidence suggests so as well. If you listen carefully to the audience on the album see if you can hear any Rainbow members cheering!

From MKII To MKIII With Love

Although Ian Gillan quit Deep Purple voluntarily in 1973, Roger Glover's departure was a more bitterer affair, having been ostracised during the last few months in the band. Ian Gillan commented in later years that to watch Deep Purple with another vocalist "is liking watching your wife with another man." Glover, like Gillan found it difficult to watch Purple with his replacement, although he attended MKIII's show at Hammersmith in May 1974 and admitted he was biased and didn't like it.

Yet, despite the way both may have felt at the time, with David Coverdale and Glenn Hughes taking on Gillan and Glover's roles, there is a surprising amount of empathy and collaboration between the pair of bass players and vocalists.

On leaving Purple, Glover initially involved himself as a producer with Nazareth and other bands, as well as a six-month spell in the Artist & Repertoire department at *Purple Records*. Through mutual associates he was approached to write music for what would become the *Butterfly Ball* album and surprisingly chose both Coverdale and Hughes as two of the guest vocalists.

When it was turned in to a live concert the following year at the Royal Albert Hall on 16 October 1975 it was a unique event that brought together Glover, Gillan, Coverdale and Hughes. Coverdale has gone on record as saying he and Gillan got on well backstage after the event and in a somewhat inebriated state discussed the possibility of making an album together with Gillan doing a side of Elvis Presley songs, and Coverdale covering Little Richard tunes. Sadly it seemed to be nothing more than small talk and never materialised.

Glover next teamed up with Coverdale and Hughes in Mid '76 for Eddie Hardin's project *Wizard's Convention* recorded at Ian Gillan's studio. Glover went one step further just three months later when he produced David Coverdale's first solo album *Whitesnake*, as well playing synthesizer and providing some of the bass. This joint collaboration continued the following year with Coverdale's second solo album *Northwinds*.

Their paths didn't cross much for many years after that, but in 1991 Hughes and Gillan were photographed together at the Queens Club Lawn Tennis Championships, referenced by Pat Cash in his foreword. In 1994 Hughes commented to the author, "Ian and I really became real friends about four years ago. I didn't realise what a great guy Ian was. We jammed three years ago. Just sitting around at a friend of mine's house. I started playing a song. And Ian wanted to compose something and I noticed he was very spontaneous in the way he writes, which I didn't think he was, but Ian has a definite thirst for writing."

In 1993 Glenn Hughes showed up at Purple's shows in Stockholm and Oslo. After the Oslo gig on 15 November, Hughes had his own gig that had deliberately been arranged so Purple fans could catch two shows in one night. Both Ian Paice and Roger Glover attended the gig, which included the Purple songs 'Burn', 'This Time Around' and 'Gettin' Tighter'. Hughes has continued to attend Purple shows and once again shared a stage with them at the *Celebrating Jon Lord* concert in 2014.

What the future holds is anyone's guess. Maybe Coverdale and Gillan will do that album of Elvis and Little Richard classics? Maybe all four of them will get back together for a *Butterfly Ball* anniversary? Whatever, there's a fair chance their paths will cross again at some point.

Advert for Glenn Hughes gig, directly after Purple's show in Oslo. Hughes went to see Purple earlier in the evening and Roger Glover reciprocated.

Glover and Hughes in perfect harmony backstage at the *Celebrating Jon Lord* concert at the Royal Albert Hall, 4 April 2014.

102

Deep Purple's
silver screen smokescreen

Undoubtedly one of the weirdest and most obscure facts involving Deep Purple regards a film project that never materialised. As early as 1970 the band had been approached to produce some music for a French film and had planned to do it in June of that year but it would appear that their work schedule put pay to it. Later in the year Jon Lord did find time to co-write with Tony Ashton the score for *The Last Rebel*, a B-grade Western starring former American footballer-turned actor Joe Namath.

The following year Purple was again approached to make a film score and this time it nearly came off. *Four Flies On Grey Velvet* was an Italian production directed by Dario Argento. According to manager John Coletta they had indeed started working on it but once again the band's hectic schedule put paid to the project, and it was left to noted film composer Ennio Morricone to create the score. It wasn't until 1990 that Purple actually produced something specifically for a film soundtrack (see page 143).

However the archives of Deep Purple (Overseas) Ltd reveal that around 1976 a film was planned with a company set up consisting of nine directors: Tony Edwards, John Coletta, Ritchie Blackmore, Jon Lord, Ian Paice, Ian Gillan, Roger Glover, David Coverdale and Glenn Hughes. The film (and company name) was *Will Adams Samurai*.

William Adams (24 September 1564 – 16 May 1620) was an English navigator born in Gillingham, Kent who travelled to Japan and is believed to be the first Englishman ever to reach that country. He was the inspiration for the character of John Blackthorne in James Clavell's best selling novel *Shōgun*.

Soon after Adams' arrival in Japan, he became a key advisor to the shōgun Tokugawa Ieyasu and built for him Japan's first Western-style ships. Adams was later the key player in the establishment of trading factories by the Netherlands and England. He was also highly involved in Japan's *Red Seal* Asian trade, chartering and captaining several ships to Southeast Asia. He died in Japan aged 55, and has been recognised as one of the most influential foreigners in Japan during this period. He is also regarded as the first and only officially recognised Western samurai, hence why he was referred to as Will Adams Samurai.

News of this potential project initially emerged in 1974 when a press report claimed that Jon Lord was writing music for a BBC series called *Will Adams*, although nothing more came of it. Anything else about the possible film is still a mystery and whilst there may well have initially been genuine plans for such a project, it is more than likely that by the time the company was set up, listing the seven band members as directors was for tax reasons. Edwards and Coletta had set up numerous companies since forming HEC

Enterprises in 1968. Deep Purple (Overseas) Ltd was intended to handle the income from overseas record and concert sales and Purple Music Ltd was a publishing company, but numerous others also sprang up, such as Purple Star.

It was also around this time that the company was investigated by the Inland Revenue. In more recent times several companies operating in Britain have been in the news for tax avoidance, operating a practice of internal transferring, or billing of money, from one company to another. The Deep Purple management companies were investigated for the same reasons and it's debateable whether or not *Will Adams Samurai* was ever genuinely something that Edwards and Coletta planned to see through to fruition. Even if it was, it is unlikely that aside from Lord, the other band members would have had little whatsoever to do with it other than being listed as directors. Then again, they might have been ready to help Jon out with the film score or even act in it? Which one would you tip for the lead role?

A portrait of Will Adams. He could never have imagined that 350 years after his death a company with nine directors would be created in his name.

In the blue corner - Deep Purple, and in the red corner - Deep Purple!

It's fair to say that 1980 will not exactly go down in Deep Purple history as a classic year. Although the band reached number one in the UK charts with the compilation album *Deepest Purple*, it was the middle of an eight-year hiatus during which the various members were paving their way with their own bands. Blackmore, now with Glover on board had steered Rainbow to UK chart success and Ian Gillan also hit the UK charts with his band. Likewise Coverdale, Lord, and Paice as part of Whitesnake were also on the ascendancy. Even Nick Simper released the second album with his then band Fandango.

Meanwhile Glenn Hughes was doing very little other than continuing down a cocaine induced spiral, whilst original vocalist Rod Evans ended up getting involved in a situation he would soon regret.

By 1980 Evans music career had been put to one side following his departure from Captain Beyond, with whom he had made two albums. He had gone to university to study medicine, resulting in a significant shift in his career path. Then residing in California, he was approached at the start of the year by organist Geoff Emery and guitarist Tony Flynn about reforming Deep Purple. They had already been involved with a reformed Steppenwolf, until John Kay stepped in over the rights to the name. Perhaps this should have been a warning for Rod, but Emery and Flynn had registered *Deep Purple Inc* in California on 27 March 1980.

In an interview for a Mexican magazine *Sonido* Evans said, "We obtained the rights to the name 'Deep Purple' in a totally legal way. I was the founding singer of the group and when I decided to form a new one with the guitarist Tony Flynn, we saw that we had abandoned that great name and decided to use it. Before this we spoke with Ritchie Blackmore of Rainbow, and with the people of Whitesnake and they agreed."

Evans called Nick Simper but the bassist was out at the time. Although Simper's wife left a message to call Rod back, Nick didn't bother. The pair hadn't seen each other since a Warhorse gig, six to seven years previously, with Evans impressed with Simper's band, particularly drummer Mac Poole. However Simper's decision not to get involved would prove to be fortuitous for him.

The line-up was completed with Dick Jurgens on drums and Tom De Rivera on bass. Convinced that it was a workable and legitimate arrangement, the William Morris Agency set about arranging gigs for the new Deep Purple. They were also offered a recording contract with Warner Curb Records, a collaboration between producer Mike Curb and Warner Brothers, the giant organisation that had been releasing Deep Purple records in North America and Japan since 1970! Didn't anyone at Warners think to question this? They started working on an album of new material at Village Recorders in Los

CHAOS AT A CONCERT.

BEDLAM IN A BED-SIT.

DEEPEST PURPLE

Deep Purple's finest studio cuts. Their loudest, brashest, head-banging best, compiled with the help of ex-Purple drummer Ian Paice.

There's Black Night, Speed King, Fireball, Strange Kind of Woman, Child In Time, Woman From Tokyo, Highway Star, Space Truckin', Burn, Stormbringer, Demons Eye and, of course, Smoke On The Water.

All on one album. Most were bashed out by Ritchie Blackmore, Ian Gillan, Roger Glover, Jon Lord and Ian Paice, apart from a couple where David Coverdale and Glenn Hughes stepped into Gillan and Glover's shoes.

All were mastered at EMI Abbey Road Studios on the new Neumann VMS 80 to increase volume and clarity. As, no doubt, your neighbours will soon discover.

EMI Records Ltd

The UK marketing people who came up with this caption for the *Deepest Purple* compilation album could never have foreseen it would apply to concerts on the other side of the Atlantic, the same month.

Although the album was released in the middle of the band's eight year hiatus, two weeks after this advert appeared in the UK music press, riots occured at the 'New Deep Purple' concert on Staten Island, New York.

However, unlike the scenes depicted in this photo from the Budokan in 1973, fans were not rioting because they wanted more. On the contrary, with only Rod Evans from the original line-up, they didn't want any of it!

Angeles. The record was planned for release in November 1980. Two tracks mentioned were entitled 'Blood Blister' and 'Brum Doogie'. The latter wasn't about a man called Douglas from Birmingham but a play on words based on Gene Krupa's 'Drum Boogie!

Their first gig took place at the Civic Centre Auditorium in Amarillo Texas on the 17th May. The following night they played in El Paso. Another gig in Texas took place the following month in Laredo on 7th June and a fortnight later they played at the Swing Auditorium in San Bernardino, California to an estimated audience of 2,500. The new Deep Purple didn't just play the songs that had helped to establish the band during Evans's tenure. "We play everything: 'Hey Joe', 'Hush', 'Highway Star', 'Smoke On The Water' - because everybody wants to listen to these songs, the audience has been great and feels good about what we are playing," was the way he explained it to *Conecte* magazine in Mexico.

The band continued gigging wherever they could. They deployed the Deep Purple logo that had been created during the MKIII period for *Stormbringer* and also used on *Made In Europe*, and used it on t-shirts with '1980 Tour' written underneath it. Ironically the current line-up has also adopted the MKIII logo.

Recalling the July gig at The Factory on Staten Island, New York for the *Highway Star* website, Marty Petosa said, *The Factory had been advertising for months that Deep Purple was appearing. There were great rumours flying around, the original line-up including Blackmore or just that Blackmore had formed a new Deep Purple. The advertisement was rather vague and when you called the venue they weren't quite sure of the current line-up. The night finally arrived and as usual they oversold the event. It was hot like a pizza oven and we were crammed in there like sardines. Then the rumour started to spread that some guy (poor Rod Evans) who sang for them before they were famous had formed his own Deep Purple and that was the band we were seeing. The place went nuts; they were throwing beer bottles at the stage. People were yelling they wanted their money back. When all was said and done poor Rod Evans never took to the stage and we were all given a refund. According to the announcer the*

B.R. FOXE ENTERTAINMENT

PRESENTS

LIVE

IN CONCERT

DEEP PURPLE

FEATURING: ROD EVANS

Thursday August 14th and Friday August 15th

INTERNATIONAL BANQUET HOUSE

TICKETS

$12.50 RESERVE

$10.00 GENERAL ADMISSION (In Advance)

12.50 GENERAL ADMISSION (Day Of Show)

Available At-"The Hall Closet" - Northern Lights Inn -

and THE INTERNATIONAL BANQUET HOUSE

For Further Information PHONE 276-4713

band was in fear of their safety and the safety of the audience.

More rioting happened at a show in Utah but many other gigs continued unabated throughout the continent. One promoter, Terry Garrett saw the band performing in Hawaii and booked them for the International Banquet House in Anchorage Alaska, where they played two nights, performing two gigs each night. "These guys have been put through the hoops legally. I went to Honolulu personally to hear them, and that's when I decided they should come to Anchorage," said Garrett.

But in reality being put through the hoops legally was just around the corner.

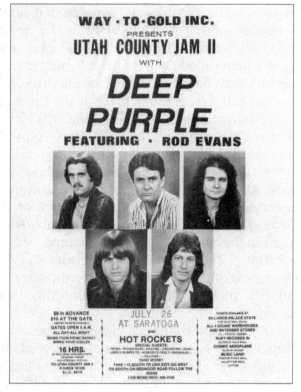

Despite playing in some of the far-flung corners of North America, word had got to the other ex-Purple members and more importantly the management company HEC Enterprises. Ritchie Blackmore was quick to respond when he told *Rolling Stone*, "I think it's pretty disgusting that a band has to stoop this low and take somebody else's name. It's like a bunch of guys putting together a group and calling it Led Zeppelin."

Despite having initially claimed to have spoken with Blackmore, Whitesnake et al, Evans was soon on the defensive when *Sounds* questioned him on his actions. "We haven't really tried to get hold of Ritchie. Whether Ritchie gives his blessing or not is of no real consequence to me as my blessing to him forming Rainbow would be of no consequence to Ritchie. I mean, if he doesn't like it I'm sorry, but we're trying."

Evans might well have been trying, but the naivety of his statement showed how out of touch with the reality of the situation he was. But he wasn't the only one who was. A Los Angeles concert promoter said, "The band has a federal trademark, and is by all intents and purposes Deep Purple. Those two guys (R. Blackmore and R. Glover) – who are with a band called Rainbow – want to get back. They see a successful thing, and they want part of it. We've got a younger look. Those original guys would be 35 to 43 years old now. The band has been in hibernation for several years, and has re-emerged."

HEC Enterprises on behalf of the other Purple members started the

Angry Rock Fans Require 100-Man Police Contingent

More than 100 officers from local police departments were called in to quell a disturbance Saturday night at a rock concert at the Saratoga Resort near Lehi.

The fracas started when the power from the speaker system at the concert went out before the main group, Deep Purple, had performed for more than 3,000 patrons.

"I think the equipment they were using was just too much for the lines at the resort," said Utah County Sheriff Mack Holley.

The power failure occurred about 9 p.m. and power came back on for a few minutes about 9:30 before going out for good. According to Sheriff Holley, several members of the audience "got belligerent" and blockaded the pavillion area where the concert was being played.

"Several members of the audience got very vocal and abusive, demanding money back or a rain check or something. The promoters had several private security personnel at the concert, but they couldn't handle the entire crowd so they called for help," he said.

The County Sheriff's office originally responded to the request by sending four deputies, but after the deputies arrived at the scene, they called for more help.

Sheriff Holley said the dispatcher called in officers from "most of the police departments in the county," including Lehi, American Fork, Pleasant Grove, Orem, Provo and the Utah Highway Patrol.

An organized group of officers in riot gear broke the blockade around the pavillion about 10:30 p.m. and gave

those who wanted to leave the opportunity to get out.

"Most of the problems were caused by a small group of about 150 people or so," Holley said. "After we broke the bloackade, only about 100 people stayed around. The rest wanted to leave."

Disgruntled concert-goers threw rocks and beer bottles at officers and the stage, Holley said. Damage to band equipment was estimated at about $1,500 and at least one police car windshield was broken by rocks.

"We know it was broken deliberately, but unfortunately we don't know who did it," Sheriff Holley said.

Several officers were hit by the rocks and bottles. Officer Stewart Winn of the Orem Police Department has hit in the back of the head with a beer bottle and required several stitches. No other serious injuries were reported.

Before the police arrived, several members of the audience grouped around the bandstand and insisted that the warm-up group continue to play after the speakers went out.

Holley said officers arrested a dozen persons, for public intoxication and drunk driving.

"We could have made more arrests but we were more interested in breaking up the blockade and allowing the people a chance to leave, so our officers were instructed to stay in a line most of the time instead of chasing after individuals," he said.

The disturbance was "cleaned up" before 2 a.m. Holley said he didn't know if the promoters would refund money to ticket holders because the concert wasn't completed.

process of legal proceedings and filed an action in the Los Angeles Federal District Court in June. By August before any court hearing could be decided the New Deep Purple had a gig lined-up at the prestigious Long Beach Arena in Los Angeles. HEC acted swiftly to try and put a halt to proceedings and placed an advert in the *L.A Times* next to the advert for the gig. It stated that the following stars will not perform at the concert and listed, Blackmore, Coverdale, Gillan, Glover, Hughes, Lord and Paice.

Nevertheless the show went ahead to an estimated audience of 6,000. Bob Ringe, the band's booking agent said, "Rod Evans, the group's singer, owns the name. There are no injunctions, no restraining orders and no box-office attachments. Deep Purple has to prove themselves as Deep Purple. It would be distracting to have the individual names on the ad. It's not a bogus situation; Deep Purple never really broke up. There was just a constant changing of people. This band does all the original Deep Purple hits."

Terry Atkinson wrote a review of the gig for the *L.A Times: The New Deep Purple band, which includes only one musician ever associated with the famous British rock group, drew enough curious and confused fans Tuesday night to fill two-thirds of the 9,000 available seats at the Long Beach Arena. The*

CONTROVERSY GROWS OVER DEEP PURPLE CONCERT TONIGHT

The controversy surrounding tonight's concert by Deep Purple—now billed as "The New Deep Purple"—at the Long Beach Arena escalated Monday when an ad appeared in the Times stating that Ritchie Blackmore, David Coverdale, Ian Gillan, Roger Glover, Glen Hughes, Jon Lord and Ian Paice would not perform at the concert.

Those musicians are the ones most strongly identified with the popular heavy-metal group. All are currently involved in other projects. The group playing tonight features only one former member of Deep Purple, singer Rod Evans, who was in the group from 1968-70. The names of the other musicians tonight have not been mentioned in any of the concert ads. As reported earlier in The Times, they are guitarist Tony Flynn, pianist Jeff Emery, drummer Dick Jurgens and bassist Tom De-Rivera.

Blackmore, Coverdale, et al filed an action in Los Angeles Federal District Court in June seeking an injunction to prevent the band from using the name Deep Purple and asking damages under the provisions of the Lanham Act, a federal statute governing trade names and trademarks.

The former band members placed the ad in Monday's Times through the firm Deep Purple (Overseas) Ltd. A representative of former members declined to comment due to the pending litigation, but did acknowledge, "It's an attempt to disclose to the public that the group they think of as Deep Purple is not the group that's playing under that name."

—RICHARD CROMELIN

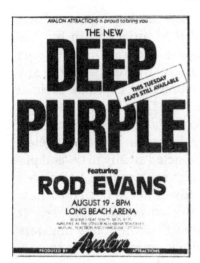

audience response wavered between docile acceptance and enthusiasm during the 55-minute set.

While Purple fans accorded the group the traditional match-held-high greeting and cheered (however weakly) for an encore, there were no cries for more at the end. Even this degree of support seemed surprising however, in view of the composition of the band and its atrocious playing.

The concert became something of a cause celebre Monday when Deep Purple (Overseas) Ltd. took out an ad in the Times stating that Ritchie Blackmore, David Coverdale and other noted Purple alumni would not be appearing at the Arena. Some members of the audience on Tuesday seemed unaware of the pre-concert controversy about the band's makeup. "This is ridiculous," cried one young man. "That's not Deep Purple up there." A woman who gave up on the show after only 10 minutes had been better informed, but bought tickets anyway. "I wanted to see if they at least sounded something

The following **STARS WILL NOT PERFORM** at the Deep Purple Concert at Long Beach Arena Tomorrow Aug. 19, 1980.

RITCHIE BLACKMORE
DAVID COVERDALE
IAN GILLAN
ROGER GLOVER
GLEN HUGHES
JON LORD
IAN PAICE

like Deep Purple. They're not even close - it smears the name of the group."

The band's playing was so sloppy that, though I believe it performed nothing but old Purple songs, I can't be sure. The group got halfway through one of my favourites 'Woman From Tokyo', before I realised what it was. I couldn't even identify a couple of others, though 'Highway Star' (the first song), 'Space Truckin'' and 'Burn' were (barely) recognizable.

Tempos constantly went awry, all sense of dynamics was absent, and the long guitar, organ and drum solos were pathetic. On top of everything, Evans has a flat, leaden voice that didn't do justice to his material. With his black tank top, tight black pants and short hair, he didn't even look the part. Flashy laser light effects couldn't hide the fact that the whole thing was a *sham.*

HEC had its day in court. Having originally registered the name in May 1968, and with the weight of historical documents in the shape of numerous records, there was no way Deep Purple Inc was ever going to win against HEC. In fact, in July, as evidence of who the real Deep Purple were (as if it was needed) a re-issue of 'Black Night' appeared in the UK, backed with a previously unreleased live version of 'Speed King' from a 1970 BBC In Concert recording.

Some Faces Are Red Over Deep Purple Band

By PATRICK GOLDSTEIN

To most rock fans, Deep Purple means Ritchie Blackmore, Jon Lord and Ian Gillan, all best-known for their work with the heavy-metal supergroup.

But none of those stalwarts will be on stage when the band headlines the Long Beach Arena on Aug. 19. In fact, no one seems to want to reveal just who is in Deep Purple these days. The group has been playing concert halls around the country despite the presence of only one original member, singer Rod Evans.

The sudden appearance of this mysterious new lineup has many long-time fans, as well as several former band members, up in arms. "I think its pretty disgusting that a band has to stoop this low," guitarist Ritchie Blackmore complained recently. "It's like a bunch of guys putting together a group and calling it Led Zeppelin."

The court ruling found that Emery and Flynn had fraudulently registered the name in California. HEC was awarded, exemplary damages of treble the amount of the compensatory damages. The defendants arguably inflicted unnecessary misery upon themselves by pointing out that one of the concerts in Mexico City had an estimated audience in excess of seventy thousand.

Gigs continued through September and although it was Emery and Flynn who had set the ball rolling, it was Rod Evans who agreed to be the sole shareholder of Deep Purple Inc and who had received all the earnings from gigs, with the others on wages. As a consequence when the damages of $672,000 were awarded to HEC, Evans was hit the hardest. Although he had continued to receive royalties following his departure from Purple in the summer of '69, these were now retained by HEC and Deep Purple (Overseas) Ltd. As Evans clearly was unable to pay the substantial sum awarded, it affectively put paid to any future music from him, as any earnings would go straight to the Plaintiff.

The album that the New Deep Purple had planned to make was abandoned although six songs were apparently recorded. Rumours abound that the tapes were destroyed although logically as HEC would have derived the money from sales accrued, if they were destroyed; it's unlikely to have been on HEC's insistence.

Meanwhile, EMI continued to release records by the defunct band. In

October an EP, *New, Live & Rare* featured three previously unreleased recordings done for the BBC - 'Smoke On The Water' from a 1972 In Concert broadcast, plus 'The Bird Has Flown' and 'Grabsplatter' from two earlier sessions. The year was concluded with the (almost complete) 1970 and '72 In Concert recordings released in December on a double album.

As for Rod Evans, "of course he was not that naïve," reflected Jon Lord, many years later. "He thought he'd try it to see what happened, but try to imagine what would you have said when it all went wrong? I only blame Rod for being silly. He should have known it was going to be difficult to get away with a fake Deep Purple. After all - he was doing it in public."

"It was not just

After the furore had died down and Rod Evans was left licking his expensive wounds, more previously unreleased material from the real Deep Purple was released, although it would be another four years before the genuine article reunited.

By which time Rod Evans had retreated from public appearances and to this day his whereabouts is of great fascination to many Purple fans.

Rod who was sued," explained Lord. "It was the organisation that was behind the fake Deep Purple who were most responsible and it was they who were hit with the greatest part of that 'very large sum of money'. In respect of that money - what price would you place on your reputation and on the right of the public not to be sold something under false pretences? And also you should be aware that these people were informed on several occasions that they were breaking the law, and yet they continued to do it. Suing them was the last option there was to try to stop them. I did not enjoy having to appear in court against a guy I'd once worked with - but he who steals my purse steals trash; he who steals my good name takes everything I have."

Rod Evans felt that he had been duped by Emery and Flynn, and to an extent he had, but his own naivety was undoubtedly the main cause for this sorry saga. Times have changed significantly since 1980 and there are numerous bands whose names are now used as part of tribute acts, and no one bats an eyelid. That said none of them actually try and pass themselves off as the real thing, although that too can be a moot point as there are bands performing today that don't have one single, original member, but still carry the name. Nick Simper who wisely declined to get involved with Rod Evans' band, has reactivated many of the early Purple songs. But he has made no attempt to claim his *Deep Purple MKI Songbook* project is actually the band itself, but merely a celebration of the period that he was a part of.

One of the outcomes of this whole episode was a ruling made by the courts that any future incarnations of Deep Purple had to include at least three bona fide members from those listed as Plaintiffs. At least now, more than three decades after the event, Rod Evans is receiving royalties again but his return to a career in music as he fast approaches seventy looks highly unlikely.

We must remain Perfect Jammers

When Purple reformed in 1984 the band talked a lot about how their songs evolved from jams. They included one of these, 'Son Of Alerik', a lengthy ten-minute jam, on the b-side of the twelve-inch single 'Perfect Strangers'.

Roger Glover told the author: "Jamming is the way we wrote (and write) songs, so most of the jamming wasn't just an end in itself but a process of getting a song written. We didn't jam that much just for the fun of it and there are only two or three pure jams recorded during this time, one of which is this piece. 'Son Of Alerik' was a one-take recording – there are no overdubs. It happened when a film crew was waiting for us to perform 'Under The Gun' for a projected video. The cameras were in position and the lighting worked out. Ritchie was in a playful mood and started the jam with (I believe) the intention of irritating the cameraman. That is why it went on for so long. After a few minutes we forgot the cameraman and just enjoyed the moment. Jon, having recently bought an Em-u Systems Emulator, an early sampling keyboard, was in the process of discovering its potential and his explorations are much in evidence here."

Given that neither the company filming it, or any of the film itself have been located, it isn't clear whether or not the film crew's cameras were actually rolling. Another (unnamed) jam was also captured at the same time, and actually was filmed, and some of it sneaked out in 2013 as part of the documentary extra on the *Perfect Strangers Live* DVD release.

Two other jams 'RIJIR' (also known as 'Shuffle Jam') and 'Cosmic Jazz' were also recorded during sessions for the *Perfect Strangers* album. They show a different side to Purple, especially 'Cosmic Jazz', which Glover has fond memories of: "It was the result of a humorous conversation about modern jazz and how it seemed that no one was really listening to anyone else. Immediately we jammed around that theme – pure mayhem. However, it demonstrates the technical mastery of the players involved, especially Ian Paice."

'RIJIR', which takes its name from the initials of the band's first names, is a three-minute 'Green Onions' Purple style shuffle. Both were earmarked for inclusion on a 1992 compilation release of reunion material *Knocking at Your Back Door: The Best of Deep Purple in the 80's* but sadly were withdrawn from it.

When *Perfect Strangers* was released some reviewers saw the album more as an extension of Rainbow's catalogue, and given Blackmore's dominance of the compositions, one could argue their case. The title track was also developed from a jam, but not by Purple. Rehearsal tapes exist of Rainbow working on Blackmore's riff for what would become 'Perfect Strangers' in 1981 but it was left undeveloped at the time. "During the

Rainbow days it was a riff that Ritchie had been toying with", explains Glover. "Rainbow certainly did jam around it but a song never appeared at that time. However, when Ritchie started playing the riff to Purple, it took on a whole new feel, especially with Ian Paice and Jon Lord playing it, and the song developed very quickly from there."

Those same sessions for Rainbow's *Difficult To Cure* album also included the band trying out another idea that was shelved at the time, and also wound up on *Perfect Strangers* as 'Wasted Sunsets'.

There are several hours of jams in the band's archive, which are often a world apart from the style one normally associates with Deep Purple. In 1994 Jon Lord said, "We've got a lot of tapes of jam sessions, and I hope we will be able to release them one day, because they'd show a side of Deep Purple you wouldn't imagine in your wildest dreams. Since we reformed in 1984 we've played more jams than actual songs, and there are some really marvellous recordings, especially from Ritchie. He plays great lyrical stuff, even jazz. We must catch Ritchie in a good mood one day and convince him, because he owns the tapes. We each own tapes like these and have the right to release them or not."

'Cosmic Jazz' is a perfect example of that and at the time of writing, along with 'RIJIR' is scheduled for the *Perfect Strangers* deluxe edition. But there were concerns from some quarters, with some of the band members not wanting the material released, as they believe it would just confuse people!

Deep Purple during rehearsals for the *Perfect Strangers* tour.
The album spawned several jams which still haven't seen the light of day.

Ritchie's Mean Streak

The reunion tour kicked off in Perth, Western Australia and the first few shows were not without their fair share of controversy, in fact even before the gig at the Perth Entertainment Centre Blackmore managed to get into the local newspapers for all the wrong reasons! Along with Stuart Smith whom Ritchie employed as his assistant for the Australasian tour, Blackmore had arrived in Perth after a gruelling 20-hour flight from New York via Honolulu and Sydney. In such a modern city there wasn't the possibility of a quiet, country retreat style hotel that is his preference, so Blackmore and Smith checked into the Sheraton. "We landed in Sydney, spent a couple of days there then we went to Perth. We said can we have somewhere quiet, we don't want to be woken up in the morning, we're up late, we're musicians so they put us on the top floor. Of course they neglected to tell us they had this construction starting up at seven in the morning and we'd been out partying until three and then they had jackhammers going off. It was horrible and we went down and complained. They had these signs up all around the hotels that said 'for your convenience' starring the construction crew. It was made up like a flyer for a band. Like they're doing us a favour by renovating their hotel."

"So Ritchie drew out this thing 'for your inconvenience' starring the construction crew, but it was like a *Monty Python* thing saying 'enjoy being woken up by Jackhammers at 7 O'clock in the morning' and he had the hotel staff photocopy about fifty of these things and he went and stuck them up all over the hotel. It got funnier from there. So we said 'look it's not fair there are no other rooms in the hotel for us, we want this to stop, at least to a reasonable hour and it didn't.' That's when one night we got to this local music store, we'd met these guys at the show and they came and played soccer. They owned a music store and they brought a drum kit and amplifiers into this hotel room. We booked a room in the middle of the hotel under the name Mr. J Sessions. The idea was at three O'clock in the morning we were going to wake everyone up and see how the hotel liked dealing with that because they were our hours. A bit selfish when you look back on it but at the time it was

Protesting rockers run foul of minder

ANGRY at being woken at ungodly hours because of the renovations taking place at the Sheraton Hotel in Perth, *Ritchie Blackmore*, lead twanger with antique rockers Deep Purple, led the band in an impromptu jam session at 1.30am.

But not for long. Although protests from other guests failed to move the group from their vigilante performance, fellow guitar expert *Eric Clapton* wasn't having any of it.

With the music at window-shaking levels, his minder, *Alfie* shouldered his way into the Deep Purple room and warned: "If I have to come back here there's going to be a stoush."

Such was Alfie's stature that silence reigned supreme.

116

hilarious. So three O'clock in the morning comes and we'd all been out getting plastered and with girls and I was playing guitar, Ritchie was playing bass and there was a drummer and we started a rock 'n' roll thing at three fifteen in the morning."

Alfie strangles ruckus

By PAUL ROBERTS

DEEP PURPLE – the rock band known for its antics in driving Mercedes Benz cars into hotel lobbies – re-captured some of the old mayhem early yesterday at the Perth Sheraton Hotel.

However, a protest performance by lead guitarist Richie Blackmore against the hotel management was cut short by a man identified as Eric Clapton's bodyguard.

(Deep Purple and Clapton performed at the ʼerth Entertainment Centre on consecutive ʼts this week).

ʼʼckmore and his manager Stuart Smith ʼbout being woken early every morʼʼy by renovation work on the 12th

21 times about the noise and ⁴ that we would not be ' to get our revenge."

⁰ of J. Sessions local music

The threat was enough, but, Mr Smith said they had managed to wake half the hotel's guests, resulting in a jammed switchboard and the appearance of security guards.

It turned out that Alfie was in the next room. Mr Smith said that he "specifically asked for a ʼ ʼoom for Richie and myself as we had just ʼʼlulu and Sydney wanted to do

"We said to the road crew who were in there with us don't let anyone in. After a couple of minutes of this the door is like coming off its hinges and Charlie the guy who was on the road crew opened the door and this biggest guy we had ever seen in our lives, just dressed in jeans comes in and muscles all over the place and just looked at Ritchie and me and said 'I hear one more note and you're dead!' So we shut the hell up of course, this guy was huge, and it turned out this was Alphi O'Leary (Eric Clapton's bodyguard). We didn't know it. Everyone said we had done it to wake Eric up. But apparently Eric was in the room next door and we didn't know this and he was playing a show that night. He sent Alphi through and he didn't know it was us. Of course in the morning, two days later we were checking out and saw Alphi down there. Ritchie was always good about that he went up to him and said, 'we've got to apologise about this.' Alphi said 'don't tell me about it I know I was woken up by the construction as well.' So it ended well but it was not aimed at Eric. I was the one who called the journalist in. We had met at the show the night before and said do you want to come in on this."

Although the threat from Alphi was enough for Ritchie to quit playing, they had managed to wake half the hotel's guests, resulting in a jammed switchboard and the appearance of security guards, a typical Blackmore stunt designed for maximum effect.

Like a bridge over troubled water

Arrests at rock concert

AUCKLAND, Sun: More than 60 people were arrested after a bottle-wielding mob tried to overrun security guards at a rock concert given by the British group Deep Purple in Auckland tonight.

Violence erupted after people at the front of a crowd of about 1000, who were milling around the car park next to the open-air stadium, were turned away at the ticket barrier.

Bottles were thrown into the stadium entrance before police, wearing riot helmets and carrying batons, moved in to clear the crowd.

An Auckland promoter involved with the concert, Mr Patrick Connell, said that about 12,000 people had paid to hear Deep Purple.

There had been no trouble inside the stadium. - NZPA

Deep Purple's career has encountered varying degrees of controversy and from the outset the reunion in 1984 saw the band hitting the headlines in New Zealand for all the wrong reasons. The first leg of the 1984-85 world tour kicked off in the Antipodes and following one show in Perth, Western Australia, moved on to New Zealand. Several days before the concert at Western Springs in Auckland on 2nd December the Auckland City Council was concerned about the forthcoming appearance of the band that had still been unable to shake of its reputation as the loudest band in the world. As a consequence they set a maximum limit of 90db, 27 lower than the level the band had attained all those years ago at the Rainbow Theatre.

A BIG BLUE FOR THE DEEP PURPLE

MORE than 60 people were arrested after a bottle-wielding mob clashed with riot police at a rock concert given by the British group Deep Purple at Auckland last night.

Violence erupted when people in a queue of 1000 were turned away at the ticket box because the open air stadium was full and they began throwing bottles into the entrance.

A concerned pensioner commented to the press, "What's the name of the group – Deep Purple? The loudest group in the world? I'm not looking forward to that." One lady said, "I don't mind too much the normal type of group. But these deafening ones..." Many residents were also concerned that the concert would attract the least desirable people and one man had protected his yard with an iron gate, sturdy fences and dogs patrolling the garden.

As the show got underway Purple's crew ignored several requests from promoter Ian Magan to keep the decibel level to 90. The council threatened to withdraw his licence to promote further shows but eventually relented after hearing Magan's defence. "Most international acts respect our requests and views," he explained, "but now and then something happens – a chemistry – and the band goes out of control."

Rock fans riot

AUCKLAND.— More than 60 people were arrested here after a bottle-wielding mob tried to overrun security at a rock concert in New Zealand given by the British group Deep Purple last night.

But there was much more that went out of control on the day of the show. The concerns of the locals about undesirables attending the show were indeed

Promoter of Concert 'Should Be Banned'

An Auckland City councillor, Mr Gordon Barnaby, wants the promoter of Saturday's Deep Purple concert to be banned from using Western Springs Stadium.

Mr Barnaby said last night the while he was not blaming the promoter, Mr Ian Magan, for the violence that erupted outside the stadium, he had failed to keep the conditions under which the council had allowed the stadium to be used.

78 Arrests

"The council should refuse to make the stadium available to the promoter and his associates," said Mr Barnaby.

About 30 police were injured when more than 2000 people outside the stadium tried to gatecrash the concert. They arrested 78 people.

However, Mr Barnaby said that while crowd behaviour inside the stadium was reasonable, the noise level from the rock band had four times exceeded the maximum level stipulated by the council.

The Mayor of Auckland, Mrs Cath Tizard, said last night that she would recommend to the council that "heavy metal-type" concerts be banned at Western Springs.

"Noise levels at peak were twice that permitted. The council had an independent acoustics engineer from the Department of Health in attendance and four times he asked a person in authority to turn down the volume because it exceeded the level. He got no response.

"The revenue we get from hiring the stadium is far outweighed by the ill-will created among ratepayers and the young people who attend these concerts.

'Lout Element'

Mrs Tizard said heavy metal concerts seemed, to attract "this lout element" who tried to break in to the concerts.

She was concerned that the police had to don riot gear and should have to be subjected to such conditions as to use the level of force that they did.

prophetic as many criminal and gang elements attempted to gatecrash the concert. Police superintendent Kevin Holland told the press 78 arrests were made. Trouble began in a car park adjoining the stadium as biker gangs and criminals drunk alcohol and took drugs while waiting for the concert to begin. As the police moved in to arrest known criminals they were attacked with bottles and pieces of steel. "There were more than 2,000 gatecrashers, well-equipped with mechanical devices to gain illegal entry," said Holland.

"We were confronted with a who's who of the criminal and gang elements. We had not seen such a collection of hooligans for years." Promoter Magan was quick to disassociate the criminals from the fans inside the stadium. "The violence erupted when the police went in to arrest these known criminals... it had nothing to do with us."

Another concert official, Patrick Connell said, "There was no trouble inside the stadium. The trouble was outside with people who didn't want to pay or couldn't afford ten dollars." Thirty policemen were injured as the violence kicked off while the band, oblivious to the events played their set.

Deep Purple never within limit

The British rock group Deep Purple was never within allowable noise levels during its Western Springs concert on Sunday.

And at times the volume was twice the allowable level, says acoustics expert, Mr Nevil Hegley.

He said noise readings reached 100 decibels, 10 decibels above the Auckland City Council's restrictions for Western Springs.

An increase of 10 decibels represented a doubling in apparent loudness, he said.

The council yesterday decided not to censure concert promoter, Mr Ian Magan.

Mr Magan could have been banned from using the stadium again for promotions.

But he promised councillors that his company would be more careful when booking overseas acts for Auckland.

"Most international acts respect our requests and views," said Mr Magan.

"But now and then something happens — a chemistry — and the band goes out of control," he said.

Deep Purple's sound crew ignored three requests to reduce the volume, said Mr Magan.

The council decided to review its noise restrictions and consider banning alcohol around the stadium on concert days.

Springs Residents See Purple

Western Springs residents hope the Auckland City Council will call the tune on volume before they are subjected to the sound of a pop group which was once the loudest in the world.

The group, Deep Purple, who held the volume title until 1976, will play in Auckland on December 2. Ten days before, the Auckland City Council will decide whether volume at Western Springs Stadium should be limited to a peak of 90 decibels.

The 90 decibel limit is a compromise: it is lower than the volume of at least one recent concert, but enough to keep people awake.

Under the council proposal promoters will lose "a substantial" bond if groups breach the noise limit.

Neighbours of the stadium last night applauded the council plan but at the same time shuddered at the news of the Deep Purple visit.

A pensioner said: "What's the name of the group — Deep Purple? The loudest group in the world?

"I'm not looking forward to that."

A woman said: "I don't mind too much the normal type of group. But these deafening ones..."

All the residents spoken to said loud pop groups attracted the least desirable patrons.

One man told how his yard was protected from wayward pop fans: an iron gate metres before the front door, sturdy fences and dogs in the garden.

The *Guinness Book of Records* said: "The amplification of Deep Purple in London in 1972 attained 117 decibels, sufficient to render three people unconscious."

The group lost the title to another band which played at 120 decibels, sufficient to cause hearing damage.
— Owen Gill.

Police hurt during Deep Purple concert in NZ

Thirty policemen were injured in clashes with bikers who attempted to gatecrash a concert by rock group Deep Purple in Auckland on Sunday, police said.

Police superintendent Kevn Holland said 78 arrests were made when about 2,000 "criminal and gang elements" attempted to storm into the stadium.

Holland said the trouble began in a car park adjoining the Western Springs stadium as biker gangs and criminals drank alcohol and took drugs while waiting for the concert to begin.

He said as police moved in to arrest known criminals, they were attacked with bolts, bottles and pieces of steel.

"There were more than 2,000 (gatecrashers), well-equipped with mechanical devices to gain illegal entry," Holland said.

"We were confronted with a who's who of the criminal and gang elements. We have not seen such a collection of hooligans for years."

The concert promotor, Ian Magan, said there were a lot of people drinking outside the gates.

"It was a running party most of the day with gang members and known criminals.

"The violence erupted when the police went in to arrest these known criminals...It had nothing to do with us," Magan said.

One car was set alight and four small brush fires were started outside the stadium during the concert.

Another concert official, Patrick Connell, said 20,000 people paid NZ$10 each to attend the concert.

"There was no trouble inside the stadium. The trouble was all outside among people who didn't want or couldn't afford 10 dollars," Connell said. — UPI

Auckland's Mayor Kath Tizard was appalled by the events, which she described as 'disgusting'. "We had no trouble at other concerts like Simon & Garfunkel," she said and put it all down to the type of audience Purple's music attracted. It was apparent that the Auckland Council was glad when it was all over and the residents could once again enjoy the sound of silence.

Purple in black and white

Deep Purple's song 'Black and White' from 1987's *The House Of Blue Light* was Ian Gillan's comment on newspaper reporting, something that most famous people have had run-ins with throughout the years. Purple is no exception, and although the papers can provide a useful source of information, they can invariably be full of fictional nonsense. Purple has certainly been victim to its fair share of inaccurate reporting. From getting the band members names wrong, such as Ian Gillian, Ian Plaice, Roger Clover and David Cloverdale; referring to Blackmore as the lead singer; incorrectly reporting song titles like 'Children In Time'; to far more incredulous stories.

In 1984, previewing the band's first reunion concert in Australia, one newspaper implied that they would be performing 'Kentucky Woman' and 'River Deep Mountain High!' On the US leg of the same tour, Thom Duffy writing in the *New Haven Register* claimed that the laser generated cartoon like graphics of Beethoven accompanied a pounding piece from the *Concerto For Group & Orchestra*! It was of course, an adaptation of 'Ode To Joy' from Beethoven's *Ninth Symphony*, which Blackmore had previously done with Rainbow and titled 'Difficult To Cure'.

One could possibly forgive journalists from a newspaper that has to cover a multitude of subjects. It's far less forgivable when a specialist music publication gets it terribly wrong. Take the UK's *Record Collector* for example. In a 16-page feature, a timeline claimed Randy California stepped in for Blackmore during Purple's first US tour in '68, and worse still, claimed that Graham Bonnet briefly replaced Ian Gillan in 1973! This was all part of a cover story celebrating 40 years of Deep Purple, published in... 2004! Hang on... 1968, 1978, 1988... according to my maths... Oh well! Don't you just love journalists?

And even more incredulous, the band's own press release for *The Battle Rages On* claimed 1974 saw a variety of lead vocalists including Coverdale, Hughes and Tommy Bolin!

The wettest Purple gig ever: Take the mud and run!

Fans in Australia, America, Japan, and several European countries had the opportunity of more than one gig to attend during the band's first reunion world tour of 1984-85. Unfortunately for UK fans, the all-day Knebworth Fayre was the solitary show in the band's homeland, held in the grounds of Knebworth House on 22 June 1985.

The same day, just a few miles away there was another festival. When Blackmore was interviewed prior to Knebworth, his typical humour came to the fore when he said; "I'm off to see U2 that day." The Irish band was headlining at the Milton Keynes Bowl, but even if Purple hadn't been performing the same day, wild horses wouldn't have dragged Blackmore to a gig by a band he loathes.

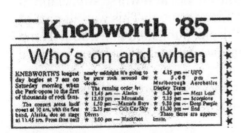

It was the wettest midsummer's day on record. Regarding Knebworth, the local newspaper reported that dozens of music fans were treated for hypothermia. Emergency services had to work through the night as wintry conditions caused havoc at the all-day event attended by 70,000 people.

Inches of rain fell, turning the arena and car parks into a mud bath and keeping twelve ambulance crews at full stretch caring for casualties of the weather. Six tractors loaned by nearby farmers were put into action to drag bogged-down coaches from the fields used as parking areas.

In all about 300 spectators were treated for various injuries and the effects of the cold. Ten people were taken to the Lister Hospital in Stevenage, mainly suffering from the effects of alcohol, or from burns received from one of the fires lit in the bid to keep warm. Police made twelve arrests in the surrounding area with only one of those arising from an assault made in the park.

Another interesting fact about the gig is that a couple of the other bands on the bill featured musicians who had been in bands with Purple members. Opening act Alaska was former Paice Ashton Lord and Whitesnake guitarist Bernie Marsden's band. It also featured non other than ex-Rainbow and current Deep Purple keyboard player Don Airey.

Mountain had been invited to the bill at Blackmore's request. Mountain was one of the band's Blackmore had talked about the previous year as one of Deep Purple's early influences. The line-up at the time included Mark Clarke who had briefly been a member of Blackmore's Rainbow seven years earlier. UFO and The Scorpions had both previously toured with Rainbow and were also well known to Blackmore.

Amongst the other acts on the bill was American singer Meat Loaf. Despite playing with a broken leg, sustained in Australia, Meatloaf performed admirably although sections of the crowd were unimpressed with his style and threw empty plastic bottles onstage. At one point he slipped on the wet stage and fell over, which drew cheers from his detractors.

Furthermore his stage time was cut short by the festival organisers, as is often customary if there is a fear of the event overrunning. As Polydor's George McManus recalled, "I remember Meat Loaf was over running and Bruce (Payne) said 'I'm going to get that fat bastard off the stage quick. To hell with Meat Loaf, my band is on so get him off quick'."

This might have been a contributory factor that inspired his song 'Rock 'n' Roll Mercenaries', which he co-wrote with John Parr and released the following year. It was aimed directly at Deep Purple. "I know this might upset a lot of Deep Purple fans, and I am sorry," he commented following the record's release. "But the truth is, it was disgusting the way they performed and did a 'take the money and run' rip-off con job."

Deep Purple performed a full two-hour set, despite the appalling weather conditions. Because the stage roof was leaking, Jon Lord's keyboards had to be covered in polythene to protect them and Ritchie Blackmore performed the entire show in his Wellington boots!

The BBC recorded and later broadcast many of the groups' performances including Deep Purple's, although for some strange reason 'Under The Gun' and 'Woman From Tokyo' were omitted from the broadcast. The BBC tapes were later licensed to the *Connoisseur Collection* record label, owned by Purple's original manager Tony Edwards and released as *In The Absence of Pink: Knebworth 85* in 1990.

One listen to the recording is evidence that Purple played a good show, despite the cold and wet conditions. Meat Loaf clearly felt otherwise and his comments inevitably sparked a riposte from Purple. "Nice chap Mr Loaf," said Paice glibly. "Somebody phoned me up and read it over the phone and I thought the guy is a fool," said Lord. "It only reinforced an opinion I had of the man anyway. Our manager phoned him up and said 'what are you babbling on about?' 'I didn't say that'."

Ian Gillan then interjected, "and do they want a fight! As if we'd started it. I think we probably did start it actually because we've got a lovely big bear of a stage manager called Brooksie. What he did actually, he threw Meat Loaf off the back of the stage. I think he was a bit upset about that. Actually it was his manager first, then Meat Loaf. They were doing the whole start-trip when we did Knebworth. He came on some of the other shows in Europe with us. I've never met the guy personally but I did hear that in one of those shows he did actually sing three notes in tune. That's not bad is it? I think he's a wonderfully large chap. We are of course rip-off merchants, which is why his ticket prices are 50 pence more than ours are. I believe at the NEC he is hoping to do well in excess of forty people.

Deep Purple with anger

★ WAR has been declared between heavy rock stars Deep Purple and the mighty Meatloaf.

For Meat has revealed that his new hit record Rock 'n' Roll Mercenaries —which he recorded with John Parr—is intended as a direct attack on the "greedy" members of Deep Purple.

The reunion show which so angered mighty Meat was played before more than 100,000 people at Knebworth last Summer.

"I know this might upset a lot of Deep Purple fans, and I am sorry," says Meat.

"But the truth is, it was disgusting the way they performed and did a 'take the money and run' rip-off con job."

MEATLOAF: It's war!

Well in excess, the tickets are going unbelievably, no one can believe it, how well they're going... the tickets. He won't cancel it of course, and he won't be ill."

Another fact surrounding the gig possibly arose, partly due to Purple's long-standing legacy of being the loudest band in the world. As with the council in Auckland, New Zealand, the Hertfordshire Council imposed a 90db noise limit on the gig. Inevitably it was exceeded and as a result, Knebworth owner, the honourable David Lytton-Cobbold was fined £1,000 by the Hertfordshire District Council.

And if that wasn't enough a local resident and parrot breeder claimed the noise from the fireworks at the end of Purple's set caused such alarm to his parrots that they took flight within their cages, crashing in to the bars. Two parrots died and one suffered a broken leg, which its owner claimed rendered it no good for breeding and he sought compensation from Lytton-Cobbold!

Despite Purple getting their guaranteed fee, Knebworth House's owner wasn't the only one who suffered financially. According to Polydor's George McManus Purple's fee for the gig was clearly very large, "I don't think Paul Loasby would want to admit he went bust over the whole thing because he paid them so much money. He would have paid them a fortune. Whatever deal went down didn't work out."

Meanwhile over at Milton Keynes Billy Bragg, one of the support acts for U2 played the riff to 'Smoke On The Water' and asked the crowd, "Who wishes they were at Knebworth then?" Judging from his experience, Meat Loaf probably wished he hadn't been.

The House of Blue Light

During the promotion for *The House of Blue Light* album from the reformed Purple, released in 1987, the band explained the origin of the album title by stating that it was a line from 'Speed King'. Whilst that is factually correct, the lyrics to 'Speed King' were largely taken from old rock 'n' roll songs, and the roots of *The House of Blue Light* go back even further than that.

'The House of Blue Lights' is a song originally published and recorded in 1946. It was written by Don Raye and Freddie Slack and first recorded by Slack with singer Ella Mae Morse. It was also covered the same year by The Andrews Sisters. Both versions were hits on the *Billboard* chart that year, reaching number 8 and 15 respectively. There have been numerous other versions of the song, most notably by Chuck Miller, an American singer and pianist who had a US top ten hit with it in 1955.

Chuck Berry recorded it three years later but his version was not released until 1974, so it's unlikely Gillan would have been aware of it from this source. In fact it's most likely that he first heard the phrase used by Little Richard, who included a reference to the song in his own tune 'Good Golly, Miss Molly' - another song title that Gillan used for the 'Speed King' lyrics - first recorded in 1956 and released in 1958.

Another quirky fact surrounding 'The House of Blue Lights' is that Canned Heat, who Purple shared a bill with at the Royal Albert Hall in 1970, released a version of the song on their 1978 album *Human Condition* and in 1998, eleven years after Purple released *The House of Blue Light* a Canned Heat compilation album was released called *The House of Blue Lights*.

Of course the other curiosity surrounding all this is Gillan's decision to change it to a house of a singular light. In a promotional interview for the album with DJ Phil Easton, which was used for the official promo LP (see page 182), after joking that the album could have been called "Born out of Chaos." Ian Paice flippantly said, "We could have called it the House of Blue Lights." And why not?

ALBUM OF THE WEEK
★ DEEP PURPLE — The House Of The Blue Light: Good grief! I thought this lot were dead. There are a few things more sad than to see near legendary stars making comebacks to the point where they become ridiculous. And that, I'm afraid, is what's happening here. Richie Blackmore plays a few decent riffs, but it all sounds terribly seventies and weary. Star rating: One out of five.

The House of Blue Light (slight return)

Purple's second reunion album *The House of Blue Light* was released at a time when compact disc sales were really starting to take off. Record companies often made distinctions between the CD formats and the vinyl/cassette counterparts as a way of boosting sales of the new format. *Perfect Strangers* had been the first Purple release to utilise this marketing strategy by including an extra track, 'Not Responsible' on the CD.

The House of Blue Light was marketed by declaring longer versions of the tracks were available on the CD. And indeed they were. In the case of a couple of the tracks, most notably 'The Spanish Archer' and 'Strangeways', these varied the most from the vinyl versions. 'The Spanish Archer' was over half a minute longer, and 'Strangeways' was about one and a half minutes longer. However the reality is merely that they contained the full versions as recorded at the sessions and the tracks were then edited for the vinyl release.

It is often argued that the optimum length for vinyl releases is about 40 minutes and this necessitated the edits, although the vinyl length for *The House of Blue Light* is approximately 46 minutes, with the CD clocking in at around 50. But the story doesn't end there. In error, the Italian vinyl release (*Polydor* 831 318-1) actually contained the full versions as per the CD although the label data had the track times listed as the edited versions.

As the catalogue number was used for all European releases if searching for this unique item - bottom centre of the back cover has the wording "Marketed By Polygram Dischi S.p.A." - that will help you spot it, whilst the labels clearly say Made in Italy. Nevertheless it shows that the length of the CD could clearly fit on to vinyl, which rather proves the point that the decision was clearly made in order to draw people in to buying the CD.

When Universal remastered its Rainbow and Deep Purple back catalogue in 1999 for CD only releases, like the Italians, they cocked up but this time they re-issued the CD with the edited tracks as per the original vinyl! "I was born into confusion," sang Gillan on 'Strangeways' although I doubt he was thinking about the vinyl/CD confusion when he came up with the lyrics.

The Beatles Connections

When Deep Purple signed its first UK record contract with *EMI*, they were assigned to the *Parlophone* label, which at that point made them stable mates of The Beatles. Although later the same year The Beatles released their first release on their newly formed label *Apple*. Jon Lord actually attended the launch party the previous year for the opening of the Beatles Apple Store in Saville Row, London. That same year, with Purple having signed to the newly formed *Tetragrammaton Records* for the USA, they also wound up as US stable mates to John Lennon, when *Tetragrammaton* acted as distributor for the controversial *Two Virgins* album.

But even before Purple was formed there were several connections. Ian Paice's first record deal, whilst a member of The Shindigs was also with *Parlophone*. And his next band, The Maze, along with Rod Evans had also been signed to *Parlophone*. Jon Lord's band The Artwoods used to perform 'Day Tripper' in their live set. But the first connection goes back to October 1962. Very shortly after Blackmore had joined Joe Meek's band The Outlaws, they played a gig at Preston Guild Hall backing Mike Berry. The support act on the bill that night was The Beatles! Two months later, and The Outlaws (using the name The Chaps) released its first record since Blackmore joined - on *Parlophone*.

Moving forward and Purple covered 'Help!' and 'We Can Work It Out' on the first two albums. The Beatles were known to have admired Purple's arrangement of 'Help!'. As the years rolled on, Jon Lord in particular, developed a strong relationship with George Harrison, with the pair living very close to one another in the Henley area of England's rural Oxfordshire.

Another interesting fact is that around the time Paice Ashton Lord had split, and before Ian Paice joined Whitesnake, Paul McCartney had his eye on

Paice to become Wings' next drummer. Something Coverdale recalled to Swedish journalist Micke Eriksson in 2000: "Paul wanted Ian to audition for Wings and Ian said "I'm fucking Ian Paice, I don't do auditions!" (laughs). Paul must have said, "Well, bugger off then!" (laughs).

As with most musicians there is respect for The Beatles. Blackmore has paid several compliments: "George Harrison - a nice guy. I don't really listen to him. When he was with the Beatles I took notice of him, because the Beatles were one of my favourite bands. But then I never took much notice of what he really did."

Jon Lord's close relationship with Harrison resulted in him guesting on the guitarist's solo album *Gone Troppo* (released in 1982). Two years later, on the first leg of Purple's reunion tour in Australia, George Harrison joined the band on stage in Sydney for a rendition of Little Richard's 'Lucille'.

The following year Lord, Harrison and Ringo Starr became part of the Singing Rebel's Band. This outfit was created to appear as the house band in the film *Water* featuring Michael Caine. Harrison's own film company *Hand Made Films* was financing it and Harrison was executive producer. The film's score was composed by one time Ian Gillan Band member, Mike Moran. The other band members were Anastasia Rodriguez, Jenny Bogle, Chris Stainton, Mike Moran, Ray Cooper and Eric Clapton.

In July 1989 Ian Paice took part in George Harrison's recording session at Friar Park, which resulted in three songs 'Cheer Down', 'Cockamamie Business' and 'Poor Little Girl', which also featured Jeff Lynne, Jim Horn and Richard Tandy. The songs were recorded for the compilation

BEATLE ROCKS SYDNEY AGAIN

By BRETT THOMAS

EX-BEATLE George Harrison stunned rock fans at the Sydney Entertainment Centre last night when he jumped on stage to play with the rock group Deep Purple.

It was the first time Harrison has played on an Australian stage since the fabulous Beatles tour of 1964.

Harrison, dressed in a white suit, ambled on from the side of the stage as singer Ian Gillan introduced the re-formed Deep Purple to the crowd during the first encore.

Gillan gave the microphone to Harrison — and the lead guitarist from rock's greatest band introduced himself to the capacity crowd as "Arnold from Liverpool ... NSW."

Gillan kept the joke going, telling the audience "Arnold" had won a contest to play with the band.

What followed was a sizzling few minutes as the band and Harrison jammed on the old Little Richard classic Lucille — with the ex-Beatle taking over lead guitar from Deep Purple's Ritchie Blackmore.

Those in the audience who recognised the now reclusive guitarist cheered and screamed as they watched history being made.

When the song was over, Harrison walked off stage as quietly as he had come on, while Deep Purple asked the crowd to "thank George for playing with us."

Harrison, a close friend of Deep Purple's Ian Paice and Jon Lord, is in Australia to launch his book Fifty Years Adrift which is about the history of the Beatles and the music of the 60s and early 70s.

Deep Purple, who were among the first of the "heavy metal kings", have started their world-wide reformation tour in Australia, 11 years after they split up.

They play their last Sydney show tonight at the Entertainment Centre.

129

Harrison steps out with Purple . . .

Deep Purple fans at the Sydney Hordern Pavilion were given a bonus — when the legendary George Harrison stepped out of the wings to join the band on "Lucille".

It was the first time that Harrison — introduced onstage as "Alf" — had been on a stage for ten years.

Harrison was in Australia to help launch a book by his former publicist Derek Taylor at a $60-a-head luncheon at the Sydney Opera House.

Wearing a two-piece grey suit and an Hawaiian shirt, Harrison chatted to more than 200 people, including members of INXS, Mondo Rock and QED, leading business persons and advertisers and Beatles fanatics who'd come from all over Australia — including one guy with a car bonnet with Beatles' pictures on it which he wanted George to sign (imagine the strange looks he got when carrying it on the bus trip from Adelaide to Sydney).

Over the last few years Harrison has locked himself away in his mansion on Oxfordshire. He won't tour any more, and although he writes songs, he says he doesn't feel the need to commit them to an album. "The whole Beatles' thing just seems like a

vague memory — like it was in a precious incarnation," he said, before adding that after his autobiography *I Me Mine* and Taylor's *Fifty Years Adrift*, he would no longer involve himself in any more Beatles' projects. Of all the ex-members, Harrison has been most contemptuous of the Beatles' myth.

After hustling himself for twenty years as a Beatle, he recalled, he didn't need to do interviews or live appearances until he wanted to.

"Besides, I think you have to be a homosexual nowadays to succeed," he quipped. "I think the record companies are only catering for the 14-to-20 year old market and forget that older people like listening to music, too."

• The Deep Purple coup of getting Harrison on stage with them was just one of a series of incidents. In Perth, Ritchie Blackmore was almost punched out by Eric Clapton's bodyguard when he insisted on having a jam in his room with friends at one in the morning. In Auckland, the police chief commented that he had never seen so many criminal elements assemble in one point, when a mini-riot broke out at the band's concert. In Sydney, Jon Lord entertained patrons of an Italian restaurant he lunched in, with a selection of old piano classics.

— SIMON MAYNARD

album *Best of Dark Horse 1976-1989*, released in October the same year. 'Cheer Down' was also released on the *Lethal Weapon II* soundtrack album.

In 1995 Ian Gillan made the point that the mixture of the individual personalities made for a brilliant combination but added, "Instrumentally they're all pretty crap as it happens. To start with, none of them would have got a job in Deep Purple for their instrumental playing. Lennon would have got a job as a singer or just as a character. But there again, they were very diverse people, from their street value, street knowledge, right through to the poetic side."

In March 1999 Ian Paice did finally get to team up with Paul McCartney, years after failing to take flight with Wings. There was no audition required as McCartney asked Paice to join him at Abbey Road studios for the recording of the LP *Run Devil Run*, released in October that year. The line-up also featured Pink Floyd's David Gilmour and The Pirates' Mick Green. Paice also joined the album's line-up at three one-off performances in September and December 1999, including a show at the famous Cavern Club that was broadcast on BBC TV.

Encore? What encore?

Throughout Purple's career there have been several occasions when the band hasn't done an encore. Or to be generally more accurate, Ritchie Blackmore decided he didn't want to! Encores originated spontaneously, when audiences would continue to applaud and demand additional performance from the artist after the concert had ended. In most modern circumstances, encores have become totally predictable, and moved away from the original essence. But when Blackmore decided he didn't want to do one, in most cases this meant, the band didn't go back on stage without him. There have been notable exceptions, such as Auckland in December '84 and at Wembley Arena in March '87. On both occasions, unconcerned by Blackmore's reluctance, the other four took to the stage and performed 'Smoke On The Water' without him.

Photographer Ross Halfin was at the Wembley show and recalled, "I was watching with Peter Makowski from behind Ritchie's amps. He was not happy with the show and kept making W signs with his hands at Ian Gillan. This meant that he might as well have been playing to a brick wall. As they finished the show Ritchie said, 'Lets do one encore and go.' Ian, who had been drinking throughout the show, poked Blackmore in the chest and said, 'You're not embarrassing me in front of my family, we're doing three encores.' Blackmore looked at him straight-faced and said, 'You're absolutely right', then walked on and started the riff to 'Smoke On The Water'. As the band joined in Ritchie walked back behind his amp, took off his guitar handed it to his guitar tech. Cookie, looked at Peter and I and said, 'Come on, we're going.' We followed him off the stage into his car and went to the bar at the Sheraton Hotel in Kensington. Not very funny in hindsight but at the time we were pissing ourselves laughing. An indignant Ritchie said while drinking a scotch and coke 'He's not poking me'!" As is invariably the case when such an occurrence happens, fans feel short changed, as did many of the audience on those evenings.

That same European tour included a date at the huge indoor arena Palais Omnisport De Bercy in Paris, which was to be filmed by the BBC for a feature on its BBC2 programme *Whistle Test*. George McManus from *Polydor* flew over to help co-ordinate the operation. "*Whistle Test* was going to film Deep Purple which for the record company was great - Deep Purple on TV. So we turn up and Bruce came to me and said 'we're not going to get any TV here.' I said 'Jesus Christ Bruce, I'll be fired. I've got a whole crew from *Whistle Test* here.' He said 'Ian's very pissed off because Andy Kershaw said they were doing it for the money.' We had this incredible experience of getting Deep Purple on *Whistle Test* and trying to get it filmed without Ian Gillan knowing." The incident between Gillan and BBC presenter Andy Kershaw

Roger Glover in Paris, just about to do an interview for *Whistle Test*, a few hours before the show. Only Blackmore returned for a brief encore.

occurred three years earlier when Gillan and Lord had appeared on the show talking about the reunion. Kershaw spent most of the interview questioning the motivation for reforming as being purely financial.

McManus was clearly not happy with the possibility that the filming might be off, "I was shitting myself because I had a *Polydor* budget to fly *Whistle Test* over to France because if we get this band on TV to a younger generation we're going to sell three times as many records, but Gillan threw a wobbler so I'm there with this TV crew trying to film Deep Purple without Ian Gillan knowing."

The author was also present at this show and recalls entering the venue via the back stage area an hour or so before the gig was due to start. The *Whistle Test* crew stood around, still unsure whether or not they would be allowed to film. Eventually Purple's tour manager, Colin Hart, told them that Ian Gillan said they could film one number from the soundboard area, with one camera only, but that they were free to film the encore. There seemed a mixture of relief and disappointment amongst the *BBC* crew.

Purple put on a good show and after the closing notes of 'Space Truckin' ' the crowd cheered for what seemed like ages. Being aware of the shenanigans that went on back stage, I (the author) was half expecting there might not be an encore. As the *Whistle Test* crew moved its cameras into place I sensed they might be in for a disappointment. When it comes to encores, or no encores as the case may be, Blackmore was always seen as the one to let the side down, but for once the roles were reversed. The rest of the band, led by Ian Gillan decided not to go back on stage - Gillan's way of sticking two fingers up to the BBC's *Whistle Test*.

Purple's production manager Raymond D'addario saw a different perspective to the whole bizarre event, away from the problems with the *BBC*. "That place is huge and they would finish a song and the people were clapping and we were on the stage and it was like, you don't like it? Because it was so dead you just couldn't hear and Gillan was really pissed of he was saying, 'What the fuck's wrong?' He was just incensed, he did not understand. We'd go 'look don't listen

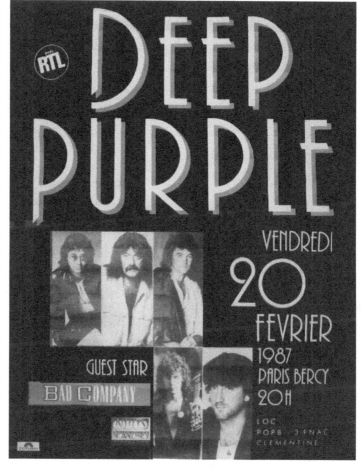

they are all standing there clapping. It's quiet because this place is so huge.' But Ian just said, 'No, fucking arseholes, fucking French, I'm not having anything to do with it.' And Ritchie went 'I think they're right, look at them I think they are enjoying themselves' so he said 'well I'm going to go out and play' but Gillan didn't want to know so the rest of the band were like 'he's not going to go out and play by himself' so him and the drum roadie played!"

Blackmore walked back on stage followed by one of the roadies who took Ian Paice's place behind the drum kit. Backed by said roadie, Blackmore started cranking out the 'Smoke On The Water' riff, then stopped, held his arms out and looked around as if to say, "where are they?" After a brief lie down at the front of the stage, thanking the crowd, and shaking hands with the front row he then walked off. It was without doubt one of the most bizarre situations ever witnessed at a Purple show; the only time that Blackmore turned out to be the only one to do an encore, though sadly so brief it seemed hardly worth it, except that he clearly wanted to prove a point. This time he didn't want to take the blame!

With the rest of the band having followed Gillan's lead, Blackmore was

COLIN HART

EUROPEAN TOUR - 1987

Official Shit®

ⓓⓟ

deep purple
THE HOUSE OF BLUE LIGHT

all of a sudden left to voice on behalf of the band. George McManus was relieved that the film crew at least got some stuff shot, but was clearly taken aback when Bruce Payne spoke to him after the gig. "I remember Bruce said Ritchie's going to do an interview and I said, 'you're joking'. He said, 'yeah he will.' I couldn't believe it that he would actually speak to anybody." For that split moment Ritchie became the groups' spokesman and the *Whistle Test* crew managed to get a few words with him afterwards in the empty arena. He was surprisingly diplomatic about the whole affair, but with his usual dry sense of humour as well, "Rock 'n' roll is built on an edge, that's why sometimes I won't do an encore and sometimes the band will. But I refuse to be a robot. I'm a very emotional kind of person and very sensitive. Sometimes I don't play an encore because I don't feel that I want to if I don't think the audience is channelling in on something I want to think about. But tonight I wanted to do an encore so the rest of the band didn't, so it made a good change!" Blackmore's wry humour probably went over the head of most people who saw the broadcast.

Gillan commented on it three years later and said, "I got all the blame for that! I'd done that thing with Kershaw and all he wanted to do was go on about the money. I nearly landed him one. I was that close. I spoke to the producer after and simply said that I'm never doing another show that you're involved in. Anyway, they were in Paris again; the whole thing was set up. Bruce said there's an interview to do. This was just before the show I found out about it. I said I'll talk to anyone but I'm not going on camera or talking to them. When I say something I mean it."

In 1991, by which time Ian Gillan had been briefly replaced by Joe Lynn Turner, the band once again received criticism after the show in Edinburgh for not doing an encore. At the end of the gig following 'Highway Star' they quickly launched into 'Smoke On The Water', left the stage and didn't return. Once again Blackmore's humour intervened when he retorted, "We did do an encore, but we just decided to include it in the main set!"

Hey Joe

The years '89-'92 are seen by some fans as a low point in Purple's career. When the classic line-up reformed in 1984, comments previously made by the band came back to haunt them. Not least those made by Blackmore in an interview with Mick Wall. Wall posed the question as to whether the band would carry on if one member were to leave. Blackmore responded by saying, "I don't think so. The band is really into each other on stage. I suppose there could still come a time when politics might again get between us."

Blackmore was spot on with the second part of his comment, but this time around Gillan's departure, unlike in 1973 wasn't voluntary. Despite what they had said four years earlier, the remaining four were now of the view that the show could go on without him. Following his sacking a search for a replacement started immediately.

Many fans were taken aback by the band's decision to continue and considered it sacrilegious. Despite Blackmore's claim that "It'll not be for money, it'll be for enjoyment," to some it could be viewed that Purple had now fallen into the same monetary trap that had forced their hand back in the seventies.

Although their popularity had to some extent already dropped off, particularly in the American market, the financial advantages of sticking together were clearly more lucrative than returning to individual solo projects. Despite Blackmore having already playfully suggested that he was keen to put Rainbow back together again, working with musicians of the calibre of Jon Lord and Ian Paice undoubtedly made him realise that to return to Rainbow would simply revert to the endless search for equals.

But as the dominant band member it was an opportunity to shape Purple even more into the directions he preferred, now that the 'stumbling block' of Ian Gillan had been removed.

Just prior to Gillan's departure they had left Polygram and signed with BMG who were upping the pressure to deliver a new album. Although several vocalists had been auditioned, none had impressed. Two came very close to getting the job - or poisoned chalice, as some may have seen it. The management of one of those certainly saw it that way. Jon Lord told Dave Ling, "we wanted Jimi Jamison from Survivor and we couldn't get him. He was a great singer and he came down at the end of January and he loved it. But he got frightened off by his record company (Scotti Brothers) because he was doing a solo album at the time and his management thought joining us would conflict with it!"

With Jamison turning the band down, another American Terry Brock, who had been with Scottish band Strangeways was the next guy who almost landed the role. "Terry spent five days with us," explained Lord. "A lovely man and a super singer. Our manager was so convinced Terry was going to make it that he got over-excited and told a few people. But it just didn't spark. He knew the entire Deep Purple songbook and he sang everything brilliantly, but he sung it like he'd learned it off the record. There was a craft about his singing rather than art and Ian, whatever his faults might have been, was an artist. It wasn't Terry's fault, it just didn't work."

Strangely, Roger Glover was far coyer when approached about the band's search for a new singer. "We honed in on a couple of singers and started having auditions. We'd settled on one guy but I won't say who because I don't want to embarrass him. But after a couple of days Ritchie said he wished he was more excited by the singer. You need a front man and a character as well. The guy was a brilliant singer but it didn't gel. We wanted someone who would let us write but had strong ideas of his own."

Whilst still without a vocalist, Jon Lord took advantage of the break to team up with some old pals, including Pete York and Tony Ashton. They toured Germany under the name of the Olympic Rock and Blues Circus. With the tour over, the end of 1989 was fast approaching and still no singer had been found. Eventually, having exhausted several choices, Ritchie suggested Joe Lynn Turner should be given a try. Even though Roger Glover had obviously also worked alongside Turner in Rainbow, he generally sided with Lord and Paice's view that the press would perceive the band was transforming into Rainbow. "When Joe's name did come up - we were in a very low state at this point because we were a band with no singer - I immediately said, "No Way! Absolutely not!" - Not for any personal reasons" is the way Glover explained it to Neil Jeffries.

"I have nothing against Joe personally I just thought it was a wrong move. I thought the Deep Rainbow criticisms would be flying thick and fast." To some extent these arguments could be nullified by the same accusations being placed upon Whitesnake a decade earlier when Lord and Paice teamed up with Coverdale, yet the essential Whitesnake sound continued.

Turner was invited to audition and road manager Colin Hart was left to arrange things. "I met him at Albany and in atrocious weather. It took hours and on arrival I asked him if he minded going straight in to meet the band and go through a few numbers."

As soon as he walked in to the room Blackmore shouted "hey Joe" and the band soon launched in to the song that had been a hit for Jimi Hendrix in '67 and included on Purple's debut album the following year.

In Hart's view, "Joe was and still is the consummate professional, and was not fazed at all. He stepped right up to the plate and strutted his stuff. Smiles all round, one singer delivered. The scene was surreal. Here was the band muffled up in winter gear in this bar overlooking rolling hills of deep snow with a tennis court just visible in a large drift outside. The heating was struggling to be worthy of the name, but at least the bar was open."

Whatever reservations Glover had, Turner certainly impressed him and the rest of the band. "Things just started to happen, you could tell, the band kicked in. Things started to ignite and within ten or fifteen minutes we were writing songs," according to Glover. "We'd try just a simple chord sequence and we'd almost have a song, that's how easy it was. Since the idea was to achieve that, the only problem in my mind was that it was with Joe. After Joe left, we all sat around the fire and had a talk and I said my piece first. I said, 'I've got to admit the guy really impressed me'."

"To celebrate we did a gig in the local pub, the Red Fox Inn, but without Jon Lord who declined to play in such cramped surroundings," explains Hart. "It was just to let off steam really, so nobody minded him being absent. We all went back to our various homes for Christmas."

The most unexpected results that occurred after Turner's appointment saw Deep Purple return to a 'proper' studio to record, the very thing that Ian Gillan had been desperate to get them to do! It was the first time since *Come Taste The Band* in 1975.

In an interview Lord said that they had recorded thirteen songs.

Slaves and Masters featured only nine, and a tenth 'Slow Down Sister' was released as the b-side of the 'King of Dreams' single. Of the outstanding tracks few are probably aware that this line-up re-recorded their own version of 'Hey Joe'. And although it was never released it was played at a BMG conference in Monte Carlo in March 1990, seven months before the album was released. It is probably the version done at Joe Lynn Turner's audition.

After one album and one tour Lord, Paice and Glover had considered that Purple without Ian Gillan was unacceptable and following some toing and froing where Blackmore pushed for Mike DiMeo but was outvoted, Ian Gillan returned in late '92 and Turner was out. A case of, hey Joe where are you going with that mic in your hand?

The Cut Runs Deep

It's well documented that Ritchie Blackmore was the catalyst for driving Ian Gillan out of the band in May 1989, and for ultimately getting his former Rainbow vocalist Joe Lynn Turner to replace him.

Blackmore was also particularly proud of the *Slaves And Masters* album this line-up recorded. But after one album and tour, Glover, Lord and Paice piled on the pressure to have Ian Gillan return to the fold.

But few people are probably aware that given Blackmore's apparent happiness with Turner fronting the band that he almost quit less than a month in to the World Tour. Having played several countries, including a

FADEOUT LOOMS FOR DEEP PURPLE

DEEP Purple are set to rock back in style with their first world tour in three years. But after 70 million album sales and 22 years on the road, this tour could be the last. Guitarist Richie Blackmore (left) has confessed: "I'm going deaf. Years of loud rock music have taken their toll.

"Every gig is special because we just don't know how long it's going to last."

Rock wildman Richie whose trademark guitar trashing once threatened t overshadow his staggerin, fretboard skill, has refused ALL interviews for ten years but told me after a packed show in Paris: "I'm not aggressive – just destructive. If a concert's not exciting enough, I go crazy."

Shy Blackmore now relaxes by playing the cello He admits: "I love classical music. It's just as powerfu' as rock – but quieter!"

successful tour of Germany, the show in Stockholm, Sweden on 1st March turned out to be one of those nights all bands dread when everything falls flat

Michael Eriksson, former editor of *Deep Purple Forever* paints his picture of events surrounding Deep Purple in Sweden in 1991: "Deep Purple used to be the biggest hard rock act in Sweden, it certainly had been in the seventies and the reunion had been a huge success as well. In 1985, the band sold out the biggest hall in Stockholm at that time, Johanneshovs Isstadion, three nights in a row (meaning that 30,000 fans saw them in our capital alone on that tour). In 1987 they had a number one album here with *The House of Blue Light*. A full-page ad in our leading newspaper *Expressen* certainly helped. When the news came along that Joe Lynn Turner was the new singer I guess few felt any real enthusiasm and then we had to wait for a while longer until the first album from this line-up came along. I think the news that the original band was gone scared a certain segment of the fans away, and it certainly meant that the news media, the big newspapers, would not support them anymore. They had in 1985 and 1987, but that was the classic band from the seventies. Knowing our media, I knew they would try to kill the band off given half a chance. Well, they got it."

This time in Stockholm they had booked a new arena The Globe (Globen) with a 15,000 capacity. About 10,000 fans bought tickets for the show and TV4 had a camera to film a few tracks by the mixing board (later aired with a Roger Glover interview). Eriksson caught the show and observed that the band "bombed". "They looked and sounded uninspired. Ritchie missed cues in the opening track 'Burn' and Joe Lynn had a cold to contend with, which took the edge right out of his performance. The volume was not loud enough for the arena and it just didn't happen. The lighting and the lasers were nice, but the band struggled. Towards the end of the main set they started to get into it, but by then it was too late and once they left the stage they were gone. Initially the crowd cheered for more, but after about five minutes this started to transform into lots of whistling and boos and then there was this realisation that the band was not coming back at all. The crowd left the hall swearing and cursing."

The media reaction was terrible - the major newspapers assaulted them like never before. Sweden's biggest selling paper ran a review with the headline "Deep Purple sink ever deeper."

Joe Lynn Turner remembers it well: "I don't know what happened but there are moments when there's nothing coming from the band, nothing coming from the audience and that does happen. Unfortunately that happened in Stockholm, which was one of the big markets and of course you can feel it much greater when you are all psyched up for a show and you run into a bad night. It's better when you do it in a little one horse town, but it wasn't, it was Stockholm and I don't think the band had the energy, the audience was just kind of numb and cold and there was no fire and I think that scared Ritchie. I think that frightened him into a reality well that's it for me and I think it was a lot of the other things that were starting to build up as well."

After the show Blackmore told manager Bruce Payne of his intentions to quit. "It was the worst concert I've ever done. When we played Stockholm with Joe that was really awful. I couldn't blame Joe, it was everything; it was horrendous. We just lost it; nothing, it all fell flat. I wanted to leave that night, I felt like giving the money back to the audience. I went back to the hotel and got our manager and said, 'I don't know if I want to stay in the band. After tonight it's all over.' And we stayed up for hours. I was sulking about the whole thing and the next night we played Gothenburg and we played a lot better."

Indeed Gothenburg was the saving grace, helped by journalist Anders Tengner who saw both Swedish shows. In a two-page article in *OKEJ*, although he wrote that Stockholm had been a disaster, he reported that Gothenburg had been a very good gig. The other press articles hurt the band a great deal, but so did the gig in Stockholm. Ian Paice told Tengner, "Thank God you saw the show in Gothenburg as well or it would have been a terrible review."

Two years later Ian Gillan was back in the fold but the band was reluctant to do any press before launching the album and tour. Perhaps because of Anders Tengner's review of the Gothenburg gig, he was one journalist who was afforded interviews with both Gillan and Blackmore, filmed for his TV show *Metallmagasinet*.

While many people were hostile towards Turner who could easily have been used as the scapegoat as Blackmore explained, he attached no blame to Joe for the lacklustre display at the Stockholm show. Although Blackmore didn't quit the band that night, it's fascinating to ponder just what might have happened if Bruce Payne hadn't helped convince him to stay. Given that it was Ritchie who got Turner into the band, would Glover, Lord and Paice have decided to fold the band or would they have tried to just find another guitarist and carry on? Or would they have gone the whole hog and dismissed Turner and seek both a new guitarist and vocalist?

Blackmore during rehearsals for *Slaves And Masters*.
Although it is one of his favourite albums,
the tour that followed almost saw him quit.
But there were a few more twists to the tale
before Blackmore did finally leave the band.

Fire, Ice & Dynamite

One legacy of Turner's brief time in the band was that it at least brought Purple's music to the silver screen. Despite reservations held by some of the band concerning their new vocalist, they had been far more creative in the studio than with the sessions that delivered *The House of Blue Light*, which barely produced enough material to fill the album.

With more than an album's worth of tracks they also wrote the theme tune for the Willy Bogner film *Fire, Ice & Dynamite* featuring former *James Bond* star, Roger Moore. Writing a film theme was certainly a first for the band, and could well have helped their fortunes had the film been a blockbuster. But alas it was a turkey.

Some fans felt likewise about Purple's song, and there is a good case to argue that. Jon Lord clearly seemed to share that view because he didn't even play on it: What minimal keyboards there are on the track were played by Roger Glover.

As well as appearing on the soundtrack album, alongside the other artists that contributed songs to it, including Isaac Hayes, Bonnie Tyler, Roger Chapman and Jennifer Rush, it was also released in the States as a single track CD, albeit as a promotional only item.

Lifetime Achievement Award given to the Bee Gees!

In 1992 the classic MKII line-up reunited for the third time for another potential box office bonanza. The timing was perfect for the group to receive a *Nordoff Robbins* "Silver Clef" lifetime achievement award at a prodigious London presentation ceremony. The entire band except Blackmore had arrived in London in plenty of time for the ceremony and initially Blackmore had agreed to fly in from New York, and take full use of the situation by tying it in with a boating holiday on the River Thames.

Rob Fodder, Blackmore's P.A at the time, booked the boat for the duration of his visit only to find out the enigmatic guitarist had changed his mind at the last minute. Fodder only found out after an angry call from Ian Paice the night that Blackmore was supposed to be flying in on Concorde, having claimed to have an ear infection that prevented him from attending. The show organisers were adamant that the whole band had to appear in order for the award to be presented. With Blackmore absent they made a last minute alteration and instead presented the lifetime achievement to the Bee Gees!

The rest of the band made public their feelings; Roger Glover was particularly annoyed by what had happened, "I was thinking of going to the launch to yell out a protest. We had all really been looking forward to getting our award." In Fodder's words, "I don't think he really cares that much, but I know that I would be pissed off! He turned down awards, much to the annoyance of the other Deep Purple members. With reference to the choices he made, I think his record speaks for itself. He would make a decision on something, which would seem questionable, but always had this uncanny knack of working out for the best in the end."

Indeed despite rubbing his band mates up the wrong way with his uncompromising approach, Blackmore did appear to have that uncanny knack of sussing situations out. After all, if the organisers really felt Deep Purple justified such an award why was it crucial all five were in attendance? Quite often at award ceremonies, anyone who is unable to attend either sends a video message, does a satellite link-up or have a colleague collect the award on their behalf.

Whether or not Blackmore was genuinely unable to attend or simply wasn't interested, his astuteness and general feeling that the whole situation was rather absurd were later born out when his actions were questioned. He simply responded in typically cynical fashion by saying "we were only going to get an award for turning up!" The band had yet to appear on stage together since Gillan's return and already Blackmore's decision to blank the awards ceremony caused a rift within the camp.

Twenty years later and a similar occurrence happened all over again.

It was announced in 2012 that Deep Purple had been nominated to be entered in to the *Rock And Roll Hall Of Fame*. Despite Blackmore having left the band a few months after the *Nordoff Robbins* incident, it was generally considered that should Purple's nomination be accepted, the MKII line-up should be the one to receive it. But Blackmore was once again quick to express his views. Speaking to *Billboard* he conveyed that whilst others thought the band's nomination was long overdue, the *Rock And Roll Hall Of Fame* meant nothing to him personally. "I couldn't care less. I would never go. I'm not really a fan of that stuff. Considering some of the people that are in the *Hall of Fame*, I'm not sure if it's a good idea, so I don't care one way or the other, actually. I think our fans seem to care more than I do. They're always saying, 'You should be in the *Hall of Fame*. You should be in this, you should be in that...' If I can pay the bills, that's all I care about." Is it any surprise, following Blackmore's comments that it was announced soon after that Purple had been denied entry into the 2013 *Rock And Roll Hall Of Fame*?

In an interview for *noisecreep.com* Ian Gillan, surprisingly shared Blackmore's views, albeit as far as his own personal feelings were concerned. "I have a simple answer: Simple to me, anyway. I fought against, all my life, becoming institutionalised. So it really does not affect me. But on the other hand, my family and friends and everyone that has stuck with us all these years, it means something to them. They love that recognition. To analyse it, and I'll try not to sound cocky or anything, I will say it as respectfully as I can, it's sort of like the Oscars and Grammies and the other awards like that - in the States, just like it is in England, and other places - these awards and honours are usually not decided by the fans, but by a cartel of influential people. These are the same people that decided The Monkees were America's answer to The Beatles. So I'm not too concerned about it. Maybe it will happen one day, but if not, my diary is full and I'm very happy. It hasn't affected our career but it does concern the fans – that's who I feel for."

Don Airey added: "I don't think the band really care, actually. It'd be nice but there's been no 'awwwww', no disappointment. The gig's the thing with this band, the next concert. That's what it's all about."

Roger Glover: "Actually, it doesn't bother us, to be honest. Someone will say, 'This is the 40th anniversary of such-and-such album,' and I say, 'Really?' What are you going to do, celebrate? We don't celebrate. The idea of being inducted into the *Rock and Roll Hall of Fame*, yes, it's a very nice honour – very nice in principle, but it's not something that's uppermost in our lives at all. I was quite relieved when we didn't get in."

"It's disruptive. We're on a course now. We have a new album coming out, a whole new impetus going on in Purple world. And that would have disrupted it. It might have got us more attention, but in the process, it had the potential to be quite a catastrophe."

"Ritchie would have to be involved for sure. I don't know where Ritchie is. We haven't spoken since he left the band. And that's down to him; he wants to keep himself to himself. I have no idea how that would work out. It might be extremely uncomfortable. It might be good. Who knows? But, it's not something that we're particularly concerned about."

Ritchie Blackmore during his last Deep Purple tour in 1993.
Would he ever share a stage with the band again?
Even if it was just to accept an award?

One Man's Meat
is three men's song

When Purple started work on the album that would become *The Battle Rages On* Joe Lynn Turner was still the vocalist. Ian Gillan returned to the fold in late '92 and has remained at the helm ever since.

But I wonder how many people are aware that there are three different versions of one of the album's tracks, featuring three different singers?

Whilst most fans were happy to see Ian Gillan back in the band, some were of the opinion that the album fell short of the standard expected from the classic MKII line-up. Was it a disappointment? Certainly Blackmore felt so, "I've done two really awful LPs: one is *The House of Blue Light*, the other *The Battle Rages On*, although that was shaping up to being a good LP without the vocals – if you heard just the backing tracks they sounded really good. Then when the vocals got put on..."

Of course he was referring to Ian Gillan's vocals. Having lost interest in his singing, he clearly wasn't happy with the end result. His disillusionment was primarily because the songs were originally written for Joe Lynn Turner and his particular grievance centred on the album's closing track 'One Man's Meat'. However there is more than one "twist in the tale" concerning this track.

But before we delve into the complex web of intrigue surrounding the recording of this song, let's familiarise ourselves with the riff. Blackmore has been criticised in the past for using the same riffs on different tracks, but if Johann Strauss could make a living out of the same melodies time and time again, why should Blackmore be so heavily criticised for utilising one of his own a second time around? That said, he had used the 'One Man's Meat' riff twice before with Rainbow.

When the *Battle Rages On* was first released one reviewer commented about the closing track on the album by saying, "a riff so blatant that I really can't avoid pointing out its *Long Live Rock 'n' Roll* origins. 'The Shed' if I'm right." Well he got the right album, but the wrong song. The riff was a revisiting of 'L.A Connection'. A riff that Blackmore clearly likes because he used it again five years later on 'Tite Squeeze' on Rainbow's *Straight Between The Eyes* album.

And he brought the riff to life yet again when working on the *Slaves And Masters* follow up, with Joe Lynn Turner writing a set of lyrics for a song called 'Stroke Of Midnight'. In Blackmore's view the vocals were excellent: " 'Stroke Of Midnight' - you should hear that," Blackmore commented to the author six years later. However, the rest of the band was becoming increasingly uneasy with Turner and eventually Blackmore accepted that they should replace him.

Although Glover, Paice and Lord were pushing to get Ian Gillan back,

Blackmore had other ideas and immediately turned to another American singer, Mike DiMeo from the band Riot. DiMeo laid down a vocal from a different set of lyrics, but with the majority of the band itching for Gillan's return, Roger Glover flew to England and spent three days working with their estranged vocalist. In 1995 in an interview with a US magazine, Glover commented, "I went in the studio with this guy and he recorded the tracks. I had two cassettes, one with Ian Gillan on it, and the other with this guy. There was no comparison."

In 2002 Roger Glover recalled the situation again, only this time he was less candid, "Sometime before 1993 RB did want to try out a singer and he and I went into a studio in Norwalk, Connecticut to see what he sounded like. I wrote a few lyrics and he sang over the backing track to what would later be called 'One Man's Meat'. It was called '24 Hours' and although it was okay, it wasn't too great. At least I wasn't convinced enough to pursue it any further. RB really liked him however. I didn't know that he was in Quiet Riot (sic) and I don't know what was said between them. I never heard about him again, until now. I still have the tape somewhere, so there's no danger of it ever being released."

Clearly DiMeo didn't leave a lasting impression on Glover who by now, along with Lord and Paice was adamant that Ian Gillan had to be Deep

THE LEGEND OF
DEEP PURPLE GOES ON...
THIS IS THE BEST UNIT FOR THE BAND,
THIS IS WHAT THE BAND IS ALL ABOUT,
AND THIS IS THE GREATEST ROCK OF ALL!

RITCHIE BLACKMORE   IAN GILLAN   ROGER GLOVER   JON LORD   IAN PAICE

As far as this Japanese press advert proclaims, there is only one version of Deep Purple worth considering although it certainly wasn't a sentiment that Ritchie Blackmore necessarily agreed with.
If he'd had his way the album that became *The Battle Rages On* would have been without Ian Gillan, but internal pressure and financial insentive ensured the band celebrated the 25th anniversary with the classic line-up.

Purple's vocalist once again. DiMeo himself also recalled the event some years on, "I did work for Ritchie Blackmore in '93. He called me in to work with Deep Purple. I did a number of songs that became *The Battle Rages On* record. That's the stuff that I like to sing you know. I was supposed to sing on *The Battle Rages On*. I had started to work on that record with Roger Glover. I only worked with them for about three months before BMG pulled the plug. They decided they wanted Ian Gillan to do the 25th anniversary. I have those same songs on a CD with me singing on them. But, half way through the set they got Ian Gillan back in the band." So not only does Glover have those recordings but so does Mike DiMeo!

Shortly after Gillan returned, Blackmore, in an interview with Swedish journalist Anders Tengner, openly admitted that he wanted DiMeo, but that he was issued with an ultimatum. "The rest of the band wanted Ian in. It was not my idea, I wanted to bring somebody else in but I was voted out. The other three said let's get Ian back. I said I'll go along with it and see what happens."

To some extent Gillan's work on the album could be seen as a session job. He hadn't had any input into the creation of the tracks that had all been written with another vocal style in mind. He was merely required to write new lyrics to fit and sing over the existing backings, although that said, Deep Purple has always worked that way and left the vocalist to work out how to fit their lyrics around the backings.

Interestingly Ian Gillan cited 'One Man's Meat' as one of his favourites on the album. It's unlikely he was familiar with the riff having originally been used with Rainbow. In 2007 Joe Lynn Turner released his version, 'Stroke of Midnight' on his solo album *Second Hand Life*. It makes for good comparison, but will '24 Hours' ever see the light of day? Maybe in another 24 years on a special 45th anniversary deluxe edition of the album!

Flying in a Purple Dream...
or be sued!

When Ritchie Blackmore quit Purple for the second time in 1993, it initially looked as if it was all over for the band. "The moment we got his letter of resignation it was devastating," recalled Ian Paice.

Blackmore had issued a five-page resignation letter to tour manager Colin Hart with the instruction to sit the band down and read it out to them. Hart documented this in *A Hart Life*, his autobiography. "I went to my room and phoned Bruce back in Connecticut. 'What's up?' said a very sleepy Bruce. 'Ritchie's resigned, he'll do the tour up to Helsinki, but not Japan. I've got a five pager from him that I need to read to you. He wants me to read it to the band individually.' 'Do me a favour, fax it right over to me now and we can then read it together. Tell the band quietly and I'll ring them once I've read the letter and thought about it. Don't do what Ritchie said'."

"I then called the others relating what had occurred and telling them that Bruce would call them individually later, so be prepared for a late night. Jon just laughed, Paicey cursed and Roger, being Roger was sad and said he'd go and talk Ritchie round. Mr. B. wouldn't even open his door to Roger, so that got him even more dejected. The phone calls between Bruce and the band went on all night. Finally Bruce phoned and told me that the band would carry on and he would find a replacement for Japan. If Ritchie was to leave, then so be it. The rest of the European tour should continue as if nothing had happened. He would fly out to catch the last day in Helsinki; meanwhile he had a lot to do."

"We were contracted to do it", said Paice. "We had no guitarist. So the only way out of it was to either renege on the deal, get sued by our Japanese promoter - who's a really good friend, and then we would have to sue Ritchie. It became very, very messy."

According to Hart, Bruce Payne phoned Mr. Udo in Japan, explained the problem and asked him if they could pull off the tour without Ritchie and which guitarists, if any, would be acceptable to Japanese fans. Mr. Udo said if Blackmore was definitely not coming then the solution would be that only Steve Vai or Joe Satriani would placate the Japanese. Ian Paice endorsed the story in 2013: "How can we do these shows? We called up the Japanese promoter and said, look, who's the most popular guitarist in Japan at the moment? Turned out it was Joe Satriani. So we said, well, if Ritchie he's not coming, if we could get Joe Satriani to do it, would they mind? He said, 'Oh, no, they'd love it.' So as luck would have it, Joe had just finished some studio work and he was off the road and he said, sure, I'll do it."

Payne contacted Bill Graham Management for Satriani and amazingly he was free. After sleeping on it, enthusiastically he agreed to join. The band were quietly told and only the crew who were to go to Japan, but with the threat of instant dismissal if they told Blackmore, his assistant, Rob Fodder or his guitar tech Jim Manngard who would not be going for obvious reasons. Glover contacted Satriani and asked if he was familiar with Purple's stuff. He said he loved the band. Roger then sent him some live tapes from the European dates.

The tour continued to Brussels and then to the Ahoy Stadium, Rotterdam when Hart was sitting in the production office, busy filling in Japanese visa forms for the crew and making plans for Japan, which was due to start three weeks later on 2nd December. Blackmore stepped into the office and as he saw the pile of Japanese visa forms and photos he told Hart, "I told you I ain't going to fucking Japan." "Yeah, I know," replied Hart without looking up. "I knew we were going, but hadn't a clue who would replace the gentleman who stood before me." Blackmore spun round and stormed back to his dressing room, ripped his visa out of his passport, tore the offending page into little bits of confetti, stormed back and dropped them into Hart's outstretched hand.

"Thanks" said Hart, as he carried on with his work. "I told you I'm not fucking going and I mean it," screamed Blackmore. "Yeah, I know," replied hart as he tossed the shredded visa into the bin beside me. "He was fucking livid, not quite understanding why there was no reaction," recalls Hart. "When was it going to dawn on him that he had pressed too many buttons too many times, especially with Bruce who had bent over backwards in the past to make things run Ritchie's way? Too many times Bruce and I had concocted white lies to the rest of the band as to why certain things had to be when all along it was just Ritchie exerting his power."

When the band minus Blackmore arrived in Japan they had scheduled three full days of rehearsals with Joe. The band assembled along with Hart, Mr. Udo and Bruce Payne in the control room. Jon Lord asked Satriani, "Where do you want to start?" "At the beginning?" he replied.

Ian Paice: "We got together for rehearsal, we set about three days for rehearsals in Japan, we did one day. Joe just nailed it. Two days, that's fine, we've got it down."

Satriani had familiarised himself with everything from the tapes and in the words of Hart, "It was as if he had been with Deep Purple from the very beginning. He went almost flawlessly through the complete show, aping Ritchie exactly, adding nothing of his own prodigious talent. Jon was awestruck as Joe played off Jon's licks and riffs as if it was the most natural thing in the world. At the end of the session, not only did we know that it would be all right, but we felt the next two days of rehearsals were completely unnecessary." The first show was in Nagoya at the appropriately named Rainbow Hall!

"We did the shows, we had a great time - the audiences didn't even think that Ritchie wasn't there. I mean that's how replaceable it is where a voice isn't," says Paice. Even though Satriani had tapes of the shows to learn,

BURRN!

BURRN!/NG LIVE 1993 SPECIAL

DEEP PURPLE

ディープ・パープル公演メンバー／LINE-UP

● イアン・ギラン／IAN GILLAN……ヴォーカル

● ロジャー・グローヴァー／ROGER GLOVER……ベース・ギター

● ジョン・ロード／JON LORD……キーボード

● イアン・ペイス／IAN PAICE……ドラムス

● ジョー・サトリアーニ／JOE SATRIANI……ギター

リッチー・ブラックモア(G)がバンドを脱退。上記のメンバーで公演を行ないます。ご了承下さい。
Due to Ritchie Blackmore's resignation from Deep Purple, the show will be performed by the above line-up.

ニューヨークのロング・アイランド出身の敏腕ギタリスト。70年代後半、カリフォルニアのバークレーでギター教室を開き、教えるかたわら、セッション・ギタリストとして活躍する。1985年にソロ・デビュー・アルバム「NOT OF THIS EARTH」を発表。87年にはギター史に残る名作「サーフィン・ウィズ・ジ・エイリアン」を発表し、ギター・キッズから注目を浴びる。88年のミック・ジャガーの

they revamped the set to include 'Ramshackle Man' from *The Battle Rages On* as well as a few gems from the seventies: 'Maybe I'm A Leo', 'Fireball', 'Pictures Of Home' and 'When A Blind Man Cries', none of which Blackmore had been willing to play.

The following year this line-up did a European tour but Satriani was never going to be a long-term replacement. He had a separate solo career, had recently completed a studio record for Sony and was committed to promote it. But for the rest of Deep Purple it showed them that they could without Blackmore.

However one of the European shows in St Gallen, Switzerland was recorded for a radio broadcast and BMG have at least one of the Japanese shows in it's archive, but whether any concert recordings from this line-up will ever see the light of day is anybody's guess.

Three for the price of one?

The Deep Purple reunion in 1984 started off in grand style with a strong album and a massively successful world tour. Press reports at the time claimed the band had received a ten million dollar advance for reforming. The band had previously been with EMI for Europe and Warner Bros for North America, and for a while it looked as if they may have reunited with their old labels. But during the intervening years the individual band members' relationship with HEC Enterprises had changed significantly, and they all had different management deals. Shortly after quitting Purple in '75 Blackmore had instructed Purple's US booking agent Bruce Payne's Thames Talent Company to manage his affairs. By '84, with Glover also under the Thames umbrella Payne clearly held all the aces when it came to offering a reformed Deep Purple to the world.

Even though Rainbow had been signed to Polygram, Payne was quick to play them off against the competition. "I remember Bruce saying to me on the phone, words to the effect, 'If you guys don't get in quick there are a lots of other labels interested as well, which must have been EMI in the UK and Warners in America,' said Polydor's George McManus.

But Polygram signed a worldwide deal, co-ordinated by Polygram's Bill Levenson in New York and George McManus in London. But McManus, although not privy to the exact details of the contract, isn't convinced that the press reports were accurate. "I can't imagine ten million dollars in 1984. That's a lot of dosh, even for then but it would have been a sizeable advance they had to recoup by selling the records. The deal was done in America with my support. I have no idea what it was but it would have been a big advance because good God you're getting Deep Purple. It would obviously have been a fair old whack and Bruce was a very good manager and he would have done a very good deal at the time."

It had been made clear that the reunion wasn't a one album and tour, take the money and run approach, but a desire to continue indefinitely with the band having signed a multi-album deal. But the level of success achieved with *Perfect Strangers* wasn't repeated with the follow-up. "The follow up was always going to be the acid test," recalls McManus. Reviews and sales for *The House of Blue Light* released in early 1987 were disappointing in comparison. "We had a top ten record with the first one but then it was never quite as big as I thought it should have been. I mean it was Deep Purple, it was a blue chip name if you like and I was quite surprised. *House of Blue Light* was number ten and that was it, it was very quick and it was gone," as McManus explains.

The cracks were soon starting to show and following another world tour, it was decided to fulfil the contract with a live album. With Roger Glover responsible for compiling it from several shows, partly because of incomplete versions where tape had run out, and perhaps also to appease other band members, some tracks were spliced from more than one show and shortened versions of some songs were also included. The record also included a version of 'Hush'- not from any of the concerts but done 'live' in the studio during the mixing of the album.

The title *Nobody's Perfect* seemed quite ironic and the record company was hugely disappointed with the result. "When they came in with that live album I remember having a meeting upstairs with all the Polydor people and I couldn't wait to get out of the room to be honest," recalls George McManus. "I had to bullshit Bruce and say it was fantastic when it wasn't because we all knew. Bruce had got the whole company together; press, promotion and everybody else and said, 'This is the new Deep Purple live album', and I hadn't heard it then. And I remember sitting around with everybody and people couldn't wait to get out of the room because they all thought, 'Fuck me what's this?' Because it was supposed to be the Deep Purple live album. It was not what the record company expected. We expected a real storm-busting album to replace every Deep Purple live album, which is impossible to do, but that was the theory, that was Bruce's theory, that this was going to do it and it didn't. Bruce thought this was going to take over from the legendary *Made In Japan* but it actually didn't do that well. Bruce thought it would be the definitive live Purple album."

The album received a general thumbs down from the press and Ian Gillan spoke openly that he saw it as an inferior *Made In Japan*. Although live albums can be beneficial to record companies as in general they are significantly cheaper to produce than a studio counterpart, resulting sales were disappointing and Polygram was left to lick its wounds. George McManus could see the writing on the wall: "It all petered out quite quickly but the financial aspects were dealt with by the American company because they paid the money. They would be more aware of it than we were and because the live album didn't sell, people at Polydor more or less said that's it. We've had a couple of albums, the live album didn't sell, and goodnight that's it. And whatever excitement there was initially, dissipated. It was that live album. If that's what Deep Purple are doing these days, if that's what they regard as a live album there's no future for us."

McManus explains the record company thinking: "The advance was obviously substantial and the record company has put out three albums. In general with a band if you're half a million away from recuperating with any band you say sorry lads we've had a go and we're half a million in the red and even if we make another record we won't recoup it. That's the generality of it. I'm not a hundred percent sure that happened with Deep Purple but it may have been a contributory factor. They would have paid such a huge advance that the first one worked in America but it was such a huge excitement and they didn't maintain it and that was maybe paralleled in the UK as well. Even though we got a number five and a top ten record it never really clicked as big as I thought it should have. Rainbow had top ten singles and were on the radio all the time and they had got a whole new audience of kids who weren't even sure who was in the band. In the whole record industry, despite these days singles only sell about two dozen to get to number one, it's still the biggest thing. If you get a hit single you get across to a huge audience. I'm sure many of the people who bought 'Since You Been Gone' had no idea Ritchie was in the band."

Deep Purple's music was less conducive to singles and radio play, and after the initial excitement of the reunion their popularity certainly dropped off in certain territories, particularly the most important market of America. Deep Purple and Polygram were at the end of the road. "I don't think our band and Polygram saw eye to eye anymore. They didn't give us the feeling they still thought Deep Purple was a current band," explained Jon Lord shortly after the split.

With some of the staff at Polygram moving over to the German conglomerate BMG, Bruce Payne brokered a new deal. 1989 had been set aside for a break from touring, for reasons again explained by Lord. "We want to make sure this album is right because we've got a new record company, an important album to make and we need to concentrate." A new album was well on its way. "There are six semi-completed and a further half dozen in a rough state," said Lord.

But during this time, friction between Blackmore and Gillan had reached the same level it had been in 1972 and soon after signing the classic line up, BMG found itself with a singer-less band unable to complete an album. After auditioning several potential singers Purple eventually settled on former Rainbow singer Joe Lynn Turner and a year down the line presented BMG with the *Slaves And Masters* album. With the reunion supposed to have been about the classic line-up the album drew a mixed response. At the album's press launch in Hamburg Jon Lord said, "I can't read the future but I certainly wish we now have a quiet time personnel-wise. I don't want to change anybody right now." Having made a considerable investment in the band BMG was keen to see a greater return. Joe Lynn Turner was soon dispensed with and although Blackmore initially resisted the other members desire for Gillan to return, it was eventually BMG that drove the outcome. Turner: "Finally BMG came in- we'll offer Ritchie like a couple of million dollars if you get Gillan back in, then you can start Rainbow over again. And if you look back in history that's what happened, they came out with that album, he wasn't even

SLAVES AND MASTERS

talking to Gillan."

With the 25th anniversary of the band's inauguration looming BMG wanted as good a payday as possible and clearly it was the classic line-up that appealed to them. So *The Battle Rages On* - album number two for BMG was delivered with a new line-up and despite it being the one the record company wanted, sadly the band's popularity in America had already slumped enormously since the massively successful 1985 tour. The world tour to promote the album was scheduled to start in the States but due to poor ticket sales was cancelled. Furthermore it got no further than Europe before Blackmore decided he'd had enough and resigned.

Fortunately BMG had already recorded several of the shows, as the band continued with Joe Satriani helping the band complete the tour in Japan. Thus they managed to get a live album and video release, both entitled *Come Hell or High Water*. The album was largely taken from Stuttgart, and the video from Birmingham. Although Satriani had agreed to step in on a temporary basis, the same month *Come Hell or High Water* was released Steve Morse became the permanent guitarist. In 1996 the band released *Purpendicular*, the third and last studio album for BMG. This period was the most turbulent in the band's history. In a mere 5 years, the line-up changed five times and BMG was in the thick of it.

It might go some way to help explain why they have released so many compilations of material combined from the three studio albums, and the live one: *Purplexed* (1998), *The Best & Live* (2004), *1990-1996* (2004), *The Collection* (2006), *Hit Collection* (2007) and *Greatest Hits* (2009). At least, the author convinced them of the logic in releasing the two concerts that made up *Come Hell or High Water* in full, which they did in 2006 as *Deep Purple Live In Europe 1993*.

The band returned to EMI in Europe for the next two studio albums, *Abandon* and *Bananas* before signing with the German company *Edel*, who have released *Rapture Of The Deep* and the most recent studio recording from 2013 *NOW What?!* This album has seen the band return to the charts throughout Europe and made number one in several countries, during a period of over 16 years which has seen only one line-up change - a far cry from the BMG era.

Money To Burn

After many years in the wilderness due to his drug addiction, Glenn Hughes finally re-emerged as a solo artist in the early nineties. Following an album commissioned by his then record company as an L.A Blues style record, he followed it up in 1994 with his first real bona fide solo album since *Play Me Out*. The sessions that spurned *From Now On*, a collection of Hughes compositions also included re-recordings of two Purple tracks.

As was starting to become the order of the day, the Japanese record companies pushed for these as bonus tracks, giving uniqueness to their country's releases. The two tracks were 'You Keep On Moving' from *Come Taste the Band* and 'Burn'. Although upon release other territories got 'Burn' as a bonus track, but 'You Keep On Moving' was included on the Japanese release only.

The eagle-eyed who bought the record would have noticed a change in the writing credits for 'Burn'. It was originally credited to Blackmore, Coverdale, Lord and Paice, as were most of the tracks on the album of the same name. Two, 'Sail Away' and 'Mistreated' were Blackmore-Coverdale compositions and the instrumental 'A 200' was credited to the three founding members only.

Glenn Hughes during the tour to promote *From Now On*, which included a re-recording of 'Burn', with his name added to the writing credits.

Glenn Hughes' omission for any writing credits was suspicious by its absence considering he was a major writer in his previous band Trapeze. As Hughes explained to the author in 1994, "I was signed to another company and I was hiding my publishing rights because they would take the lot." It was a catch 22 situation as he clearly explained and although he wasn't receiving publishing royalties he was at least getting sales royalties although these are never as lucrative, but because he wasn't able to put his name to any of the songs, it was agreed he would receive a larger share of sales royalties for that album to compensate in some way.

"*Burn* has kept me going all these years," he said at the time of the release of *From Now On*. "*Burn* has sold over four and a half million copies. Thank God for that, it's the album that keeps me going."

Once free of his earlier publishing deal he was then able to once again put his name to the composition credits to the songs from *Burn* that he helped contribute to, including the title track, re-recorded for *From Now On*. When *Burn* was reissued in 2004, in a remastered and expanded format the omission that had been there for twenty years was finally rectified and Hughes also received songwriting credits for 'Might Just Take Your Life', 'Lay Down, Stay Down', 'You Fool No One' and 'What's Goin' On Here'.

The remaster sold well and the increase in earnings from publishing royalties will have given Glenn more money to burn. Fortunately these days, for a man who reckons he blew a million dollars on cocaine in his dark years, he now prefers to spend his money on sharp clothes and a nice Jaguar car for cruising around in the Los Angeles area where he currently resides.

Going for a song?

Even though Ritchie Blackmore is synonymous with playing Fender Stratocasters, initially his instrument of choice was a cherry red Gibson ES-335. He had purchased the guitar in 1961 when he turned professional and used it exclusively until he was given an Eric Clapton Fender cast-off from Clapton's roadie. He continued to then use both the Fender and the Gibson for the next three years. On record the last time he played the Gibson was *In Rock*, and in particular the astonishing solo on 'Child in Time'. Live he continued to play it until summer 1971 for the instrumental 'Wring That Neck' and when that was replaced in the set with 'Lazy' he used Fenders exclusively. But he did use it one more time in December that year. While Purple was in Montreux recording *Machine Head* they were suddenly required to drop everything and fly back to London to appear on the BBC weekly music show *Top of the Pops* to perform 'Fireball'.

To travel back with their instruments wasn't an option, so Ritchie grabbed the Gibson from his home for the TV performance. From that point on the guitar remained at his home. Years later the author asked him if he still had it, to which he replied, "I think the second wife has it." It certainly indicated at the time that he had no emotional attachment to it, although that has changed to some degree as the years have rolled on.

However, Babs, his second wife did keep the guitar after they split in the mid seventies, and on 7 September 1995 she finally decided to sell it by auction. It went under the hammer at Christie's in London for £5,625. Babs told the author she thought it was bought for the *Hard Rock Café* in Amsterdam where she thinks it was displayed. However nine years later it was back at Christie's and auctioned off again by the previous purchaser. This time it reached £15,535 on 29 September 2004. An English guitar dealer based in California purchased it. Some months on and a keen Blackmore fan tracked down the dealer and in his own words, "I was very lucky and paid the price of a *Porsche* for it. And my wife let me. It was definitely a mid-life crisis."

The biggest irony to all this is that despite

Blackmore having moved to the States in the mid-seventies and now residing in Long Island, New York, the guitar now resides with its current owner, a mere 50 miles from Blackmore's current home!

Ritchie Blackmore performing in the early days of Purple with his Gibson ES-335.
When 'Wring That Neck' was dropped from the set in 1971, the Gibson was no longer required.

Sometimes I Feel Like Screaming

O ne of the most astonishing stories in Deep Purple's long and illustrious career occurred in Chile in 1997. South America was at that point a relatively untapped market for Western rock music. The Joe Lynn Turner fronted line-up had played a few shows in Brazil in 1991, but this was the first time Purple had done a full scale South American tour that also included Argentina, Brazil, Peru and Bolivia.

But it all kicked off with one show in the Chilean capital of Santiago. A show that will be remembered for all the wrong reasons and that made headlines around the world. The show took place at the Santa Laura football stadium on 27 February. It was full to capacity with 20,000 Chileans witnessing Purple for the first time.

For this tour they opened the shows with 'Hush'. It was followed by 'Fireball', and aptly, the third number was 'Into the Fire', which is when sparks began to fly. However, not with the band, but as a result of over enthusiastic fans, revelling in their first experience of a Purple gig. Several had scaled one of the lighting rigs in order to get a better view. Unfortunately during 'Into the Fire' the additional weight was too much for the rig to take and it suddenly collapsed. Sparks were flying as the lighting tower crashed to the ground, but miraculously no one died. The concert was halted

Fans injured as tower collapses

SANTIAGO, Chile (AP) — A light tower collapsed during a concert by the British rock band Deep Purple after several fans climbed it. Forty-four people were injured, some seriously.

TV showed firefighters taking injured spectators from the scene Thursday night. Santiago officials said yesterday that 44 people were injured.

Several fans climbed the metal light tower in the 20,000-seat Santa Laura soccer stadium, causing it to collapse, the witnesses said.

The concert was suspended for about 40 minutes, and outside the stadium, police used water cannons to scatter dozens of youths who — apparently unaware of the accident — demanded to be let inside. Authorities later allowed the concert to resume.

as the 44 people injured were rescued from the wreckage.

Steve Morse commented on his observations: "I watched the entire PA and lighting tower buckle and fall in to the crowd as if in slow motion. There were at least sixty guys who had climbed up to get a better view and now they were leaping in to the rows of innocent people below to break their fall. Within a few seconds there was a huge jet of sparks as the high-voltage power lines near the collapsing framework were cut and shorted. I held my breath waiting to see if our light and sound guys would make it out of there without being burned or electrocuted."

Although Ian Gillan spoke through his microphone to try and ensure everyone kept calm, the main sound system was out of action and much of the stadium was in darkness as the band were ushered back to their dressing rooms. Once they had established that their crewmembers were safe and that no one had died or was critically injured the band felt more relaxed.

Although clearly shocked by what had happened Purple considered the possibility of continuing with the show. After about 40 minutes, with the injured taken to hospital and a new makeshift lighting rig set up, and after consultation with the police, the promoters decided that it would be more dangerous to cancel the show with 20,000 hungry fans in the stadium than it would to continue.

"The stadium was still full," Morse recalled. "The sound and light boards were dead so we ran the PA off the monitor mix, wired a bank of lights and went back on." Despite what had already happened it didn't dampen the spirits of the audience as Morse explains: "The place went complete bonkers with this kind of violent mosh pit in full force near the front of the stage. Security was spending all their time throwing water at these people being

TOWER HOLDING LOUDSPEAKERS COLLAPSES AT DEEP PURPLE CONCERT AND INJURES 20 PEOPLE

At least 20 people were injured at a rock concert on Thursday when a tower holding speakers collapsed at the start of a Deep Purple gig in Chile, officials said.
Initial reports from the fire department and local media did not indicate how many people were injured and if there were fatalities.
The tower collapsed under the weight of a crowd that had climbed to see the band, which had only played three songs when the show was suspended.
It fell on top of people sitting at Santa Laura Stadium in the northern part of Santiago.

trapped and crushed at the front of the stage. Any females or couples had long since abandoned this war zone in front of us."

The audience's exuberance was to a degree to be expected but nothing could prepare Steve Morse for what followed. "I bent down to beg a security man to stop this brain-dead guy from spitting at the band. He just asked me for a guitar pick and did nothing else. If you are like me, having someone spit at you is a huge insult, right? Apparently in Chile it is expected, somewhat tolerated and even construed as a twisted, aggressive form of approval."

This was the explanation that Morse received from several people after the show. Interestingly Blackmore's reformed Rainbow had played in Chile for the first time a few months prior to the Purple gig. Their show was broadcast on radio there and vocalist Doogie White can be clearly heard telling the crowd to stop spitting. Ian Gillan had also played in Chile a few years earlier during the period where Purple had sacked and replaced him with Turner. If Gillan or anyone from the Blackmore entourage had informed the rest of the Purple guys in advance of what to expect, it begs the question, would they have still opted to do the gig?

An interesting thought, but alas they clearly were not prepared for this Chilean hospitality custom. "Imagine playing a solo with your eyes closed," said Morse, "and suddenly finding your face is splattered with someone else's spit. Ian, who had been in the same situation years before, walked over and wiped my face with a towel without missing a beat." Unfortunately for Morse as he opened his eyes he motioned to the group in front of him to point out the culprit, but they just took that as Morse wanting to acknowledge his approval to the man responsible!

Morse soldiered on in his usual professional manner as the spitting continued throughout the gig. As the final encore number 'Highway Star' had finished Morse made eye contact with the spitter and gave the security men something to react to at last. "I went down in to the pit heading for my new 'friend'. As my left hand was in motion and just a few inches away from showing my appreciation the comatose security guys suddenly had something to do."

Before he knew it, Morse had both arms immobilised and someone who he suspects was the spitter was holding his neck, whilst someone else ripped off a memento from his necklace. Despite this unfortunate incident Morse thought that the majority of the crowd were fantastic and two years later Purple returned to the same venue as part of another South American tour. On that occasion it was filmed for Chilean TV and nothing untoward happened. The set list had changed, and the classic *Purpendicular* track 'Sometimes I Feel Like Screaming' was back in the show. But it was Morse's experiences the first time in Chile that really made him feel like screaming.

The Rolling Stones
Connections

O f the principle bands that emerged in the sixties, it goes without saying that The Beatles were the most influential – acknowledged by Purple with covers on the first two albums. But from the outset they also acknowledged The Stones with their instrumental version of 'Paint it, Black' which included Paice's drum solo. It was part of the live set from the first show and remained a part of the stage act until' 71. It was brought back for the 25th anniversary tour in 1993 as a relatively brief rendition with no drum solo, and with vocals for the first time, even though Ian Gillan hadn't exactly learnt them and just meandered his way through it!

It's somewhat surprising that the band ever covered a Stones number in the first place given Blackmore's often-dismissive comments towards them. "I'm not into that Keith Richards trip of having all those guitars in different tunings. I never liked the Rolling Stones much anyway," he said in one interview. In another he suggested their popularity was to do with more than the music.

It's possible that their was a degree of professional jealousy towards The Stones, whom he first encountered in 1964 when his then band The Outlaws supported them in Salisbury. In those days they were often just given details of where and when to play, but little else. They were initially excited to turn up at the venue to find hundreds of screaming girls only to discover The Stones were headlining and the girls weren't there for them!

City Hall - Salisbury

WEDNESDAY, MARCH 18th

The Rolling Stones

THE and JOHNNY
OUTLAWS QUANTROSE '5'

Tickets are Selling Fast — Get yours NOW from
TED HARDY'S. 24 b MILFORD STREET - ADMISSION 7/6

Jon Lord also had connections with The Stones before Purple through his band The Artwoods who were fronted by Art Wood, older brother of future Stone's guitarist Ronnie Wood. In fact Lord briefly played in Santa Barbera Machine Head, a recording band with Ronnie, shortly after The Artwoods.

In 1969 press reports claimed that Purple were going to tour the States as support to the Stones, but it never materialised. It could have been interesting if it had gone ahead and Purple had played 'Paint it, Black' before the headlining band took to the stage!

By the seventies Purple were just one of numerous bands who employed the Rolling Stones Mobile Studio, which we all know they immortalised in the lyrics to 'Smoke On The Water'. One of the more bizarre

DEEP PURPLE
A TOUR WITH THE ROLLING STONES?

AND while the rain falls in Britain, Deep Purple look out of their windows in America and the sun is shining a spotlight upon them because there, in the space of a few short months hit records happen and they earn money and praise is received.

A "Hush" rush up the charts started it all off for them in the U.S. and they followed it up with a short tour of which every critic before seeing Deep Purple said "manufactured teenybopper group" because they'd had a hit promoted heavy by Tetragrammaton and never been heard live, but after seeing Deep Purple said "great group full of talent". And the group returned to this country where few people seem to know who they are, and they hope to convert, before going back across the Giant Atlantic Puddle once more this time, perhaps, to tour with the Rolling Stones.

When they arrived in America, Americans had heard and bought their record and "Deep Purple" was a name known but little else. "We were put in a difficult position," said organist Jon Lord, "in that we really felt we had to prove ourselves—work hard to be accepted."

happened that they were more than accepted, viz., for

connections was a Glenn Hughes vocal session with Al Kooper, Little Feat's Richie Hayward and Jeff Baxter from the Doobie Brothers. They recorded an album of covers in disco style under the name of *Four on the Floor*. Side 2 was called the 'Glimmer Twins Medley' and featured 'Let's Spend The Night Together', 'Lady Jane', 'Paint It, Black' and 'Under My Thumb'. As with Purple, 'Paint It, Black' was done as an instrumental but Hughes sung on the other three numbers. It wasn't the first time Hughes had sung Rolling Stones songs, as his first band The Hooker Lees, performed several Stones' numbers in 1966.

Joe Satriani, who stepped in following Blackmore's departure in 1993 to help the band fulfil a Japanese tour, and a European tour the following year, had previously been a member of Mick Jagger's band for the Stones vocalist's debut solo tour in 1988.

In a conversation with Roger Glover, Ian Gillan said, "a band is something that is made up of a collective consciousness of five people or however many there is. What is it they say about the sum being greater than the total of the parts? You can just look at the Rolling Stones. You wouldn't actually probably think of any of those guys necessarily as great individual performers, and yet together they shine, absolutely brilliant."

The Led Zeppelin
Connections

Like it or not, for many people Purple are often thought of in the same breath as both Led Zeppelin and Black Sabbath. Although the author would argue that all three bands are vastly different, the fact that they all started to achieve success around the same time did ensure that journalists often compared them. Possibly the first connection comes from a comment made by Blackmore who claims he did a session in the sixties with Jeff Beck that was produced by Jimmy Page. Given Blackmore's penchant for throwaway comments and wind-ups, this could well be another designed to lead people up a blind alley, although he has repeated this story many times throughout the years. When the author met Page in 2013 the Zeppelin guitarist was adamant he had never worked with Blackmore. The memory of one of them must be wrong but for the time being this particular little anecdote remains ambiguous.

However they have crossed paths many times over the years, particularly in the mid seventies after Purple had moved to California as tax exiles. Both Zeppelin and Purple hung around the rock 'n' roll haunts such as the *Rainbow Bar & Grill* on Sunset Strip in Los Angeles. 1976 was a year in particular when the members of Zeppelin and Purple were often hanging around together. A drunken John Bonham got up on stage at Purple's gig at the Radio City Music Hall in New York in January to plug Zeppelin's then forthcoming film *The Song Remains The Same*. Bonham had a friendship with Glenn Hughes that stretched back to Hughes' time in Trapeze. Both hail from the same West Midlands area of England and Bonham was a big fan of Trapeze. Like Bonham and Hughes, Robert Plant is also from the West Midlands and was also in attendance at the Radio City Music Hall gig, hanging around backstage after the show.

When Blackmore was asked in an interview in 1999 if he ever had anything to do with Led Zeppelin he replied, "I used to know Robert very well, and John Bonham would come to our rehearsals and sit in on drums." Indeed, in May '76 Bonham spent some time with Blackmore, who by then was preparing his new band Rainbow for a world tour. Bonham attended the rehearsals and played with the band on 'Man On The Silver Mountain', a song that he absolutely loved. So much so that when he gatecrashed an upmarket party Blackmore was hosting around the same time he took Bach off the record player and replaced it with his favourite record of the moment.

In 1991 a coming together of Purple and Zeppelin occurred when David Coverdale and Jimmy Page surprised the rock world and united for an album. They also completed one Japanese tour before folding the project. Those live dates saw Coverdale singing several Led Zeppelin songs in a set that also included some of his Whitesnake numbers, but no Purple tunes.

The pairing did little to impress Robert Plant who had already had a public spat with Coverdale who he had criticised in 1987 following the release of Whitesnake's 'Still of the Night'. Plant felt that Coverdale was re-inventing himself by adopting Plant's style and considered the song as a copy of Zeppelin. Although the words black, kettle and pot do spring to mind when copying accusations come from the Zeppelin camp! Similar accusations were thrown at Purple that 'Perfect Strangers' was a copy of Zeppelin's 'Kashmir', a track that Blackmore has acknowledged with admiration. The battle rages on with regards to that.

It was something that Blackmore expanded upon when talking to journalist Neil Jeffries in 1995, "I used to be very friendly with Bonzo. We'd be sitting in the Rainbow and he'd be really up and drunk or really depressed, but we'd be sitting there drinking and he'd be looking at the table. And he used to say to me: 'It must be really hard to stand there and go der-der-derr, der-der, de-derr ('Smoke On The Water').' 'Yeah, it's nearly as difficult as going duh-der duh-der dum ('Whole Lotta Love'). At least we don't copy anybody!' 'What are you talking about? That's bullshit! I know exactly where you got duh-der duh-der dum from; you got it from 'Hey Joe', you just put it to a rhythm.' And he's thinking... 'And 'Immigrant Song' was 'Little Miss Lover'.' 'What are you talking about?' 'Bom-bobba-didom ba-bom bobbadidom...' He was not a happy man, but he started it. We then went upstairs to the toilet. We're both there, weeing away, and he says: 'Rich, did you mean all that?' 'No, not really, I was just having a go back at you.' 'Oh. I didn't mean it either. There's room at the top for everybody.' So we carried on weeing, then went back downstairs and started drinking again. But he loved it, he was the kind of guy who liked confrontation, and I would always give it to him. But I always remember when he said that, thinking how we'd taken bits and pieces from people, so I told him where he got his stuff from. It was interesting to see how his mind was going: 'Pagey, you bastard, now I know'."

But from the Purple side of things it's generally been nothing but compliments. When the author interviewed Jon Lord in 2007 he said, "I played with Robert Plant last year when we did the *Sunflower Jam* and that was a real buzz. I've always liked what Percy does. I think it's terrific stuff."

That same year, on 22 May 2006, Jon Lord appeared at Sweden's *Polar Music Prize* awards ceremony, held in the presence of the Swedish King. He made a brief speech and presented the *Polar Lifetime Achievement* award to Page, Plant, Jones and Zoe Bonham.

In more recent times musicians from both bands have also played each other's material. Ian Paice has played 'Whole Lotta Love' with Italian band Odessa. John Paul Jones played 'Black Night' with Paice, Brian May, Bruce Dickinson and Brian Auger at the 2012 *Sunflower Jam*, with foreword writer Pat Cash in the audience. While Steve Morse has regularly played the 'Whole Lotta Love' riff at Purple shows throughout the years before cranking out 'Smoke On The Water'. Deep Zeppelin or Led Purple?

The Black Sabbath
Connections

IAN GILLAN, Deep Purple's singer, hit back this week at "underground snobbery" and all the knocking that exists when a band finally makes it. He defended success in the singles' chart and he defended Purple's fans. He even stood-up for Black Sabbath.

ˠᵃn knows there's not much really brings us down. It

L ike Zeppelin, there are many connections with Black Sabbath. To start with, at the height of their popularity both bands were part of the bill for the all-day California Jam in 1974. In Glenn Hughes autobiography Tony Iommi said, "I watched some of their set, and Glenn stood out. His talent was remarkable." As with Hughes's relationship with Zeppelin's Bonham and Plant, likewise he and Iommi had grown up in the same area and Hughes had known the Sabbath guys from way back. The night before the California Jam, Hughes, Iommi and Ozzy Osbourne partied together.

As time moved on Hughes became one of two Deep Purple members who spent time fronting Sabbath. The other being Ian Gillan whose year long sabbatical after joining Sabbath in 1983 surprised many at the time, including Gillan himself who agreed to it after a drinking session in the Bear in Oxford with Tony Iommi and Geezer Butler. It was a union that divided opinions of the fan bases of both bands. The resulting *Born Again* album also had a mixed reception but it was when the band went on the road that the fans loyalty was fully tested.

Gillan struggled to remember the words to the earlier Sabbath classics, originally sung by Ozzy Osbourne, and fans were also surprised that the band included 'Smoke On The Water' for the encores. Following one world tour they agreed to call it a day and shortly after it the Deep Purple reunion saw Gillan back in his rightful place. Nearly a decade later, Gillan said, "I was the worst singer Black Sabbath ever had. It was totally, totally incompatible with any music they'd ever done. I

Gillan
of Black
Sabbath

'Revitalized' Black Sabbath group goes back on the road

didn't wear leathers; I wasn't of that image... I think the fans probably were in a total state of confusion."

Sabbath all but folded and Tony Iommi worked on a solo album, but he couldn't resist luring into his fold the former Purple man who had impressed him a decade earlier. Glenn Hughes did all the vocals for Iommi's *Seventh Star* album recorded in 1985 and released in January '86. Due to record company pressure it was released as Black Sabbath featuring Tony Iommi. The Sabbath man's next move was to tour to promote the album as Black Sabbath with Hughes fronting it. "Until they come and see this new band," said Hughes, "there is a definite tinge of dinosaurism. But what I think I've done with Sabbath is update the sound a little on the album. We'll be doing a lot of the old songs on tour, but there's going to be a definite contemporary air. I'm going to try to deliver a little more theatrical content, a little more flash, a little bit more dynamics- rather than your overall doom, death and whatever. Although it'll still be menacing enough for kids who want to come and be menaced."

Unfortunately for Hughes it was his cocaine addiction that was menacing and four days before the start of the tour he had a fight with the band's production manager John Downing that splintered his orbital bone. The injury affected his ability to sing and after only five shows in the States in March '86 he had to bail out.

When Sabbath reached the UK two months later with new singer Ray Gillen, they were still selling t-shirts with Hughes face on them! Hughes later said "singing for Black Sabbath was like James Brown fronting Metallica" and clearly felt at odds with Sabbath's style. But despite that, he has at times during his solo shows performed some of the songs from the

'Let's do the big one first.

Sabbath's lineup today consists of Iommi, Hughes, drummer Eric Singer, bassist Dave Spitz and keyboard player Geoff Nichols. As Hughes sees it, one of his contributions to Sabbath has been to update the band's style and counteract any tendency on the part of audiences to view the band as strictly a '70s holdover.

"Until they come and see this new band," says Hughes, "there is a definite tinge of dinosaurism. But I think what I've done with Sabbath is update the sound a little on the album. We'll be doing a lot of the old songs on tour, but there's going to be a definite contemporary air. I'm going to try to deliver a little more theatrical content, a little more flash, a little bit more dynamics--rather than your overall doom, death and whatever. Although it'll still be menacing enough for kids who want to come and be menaced.

"We'll be using extra lighting. There's going to be a lot of use of lasers. Black Sabbath was never really a band to use much stage lighting. It was basically, 'Let's get onstage, and let's get off.' I'm trying to help, as much as I can, by introducing things most bands are doing now."

Hughes, who has worked with Deep Purple and Trapeze, un-

album.

In 1989 Iommi and Gillan teamed up again for a charity recording of 'Smoke On The Water' with an all-star cast that also included Blackmore. Despite the problems encountered from their first collaboration, Iommi's admiration for Hughes's voice resulted in a second album, *Fused*, recorded in 2004 and released the following year. By this time Hughes had been sober from drink and drugs for a decade.

Ian Gillan also teamed up again with Iommi to record a charity single 'Out of My Mind' in 2011, which also featured Jon Lord. A compilation album *Who Cares* that included a selection of tracks by both artists, separately and together, followed it, most of which were from previous projects. But the album also included a version of 'Trashed' from *Born Again* performed by Gillan, Iommi, Ian Paice and Roger Glover. Other tracks on the album included an acoustic version of 'When A Blind Man Cries' by Gillan with Steve Morse and 'Let It Down Easy' by Iommi and Glenn Hughes from the *Fused* album, previously only available as a bonus track on the Japanese release.

Another connection comes in the form of Purple's engineer and producer Martin Birch who produced the two Sabbath albums *Heaven And Hell* and *Mob Rules* during the period when Blackmore's former Rainbow frontman Ronnie James Dio had taken over from Ozzy Osbourne. And if that wasn't enough, following Dio's departure, in 1982, according to *Kerrang!* magazine, Coverdale was considered for the vocalist position with Black Sabbath although this hasn't been substantiated.

Sabbath's career has arguably been even rockier than Purple's, and just as Ian Gillan has had three stints as Purple's vocalist, Ronnie Dio did likewise with Sabbath although the last time it was under the Heaven and Hell moniker. Following Dio's death Glenn Hughes once again shared a stage along with Tony Iommi and Geezer Butler under the Heaven and Hell name as a tribute to Dio at the 2010 *High Voltage Festival*. But I wonder how many people know that there was also a Zeppelin member on the stage that night? Jimmy Page, who watched the show from the wings.

December is a cruel time

Inspired by *The Waste Land* by T.S Elliot, Jon Lord wrote that, "April is a cruel time" in the 1969 composition 'April' that appeared on the band's third album *Deep Purple*. However, it was December that would prove to be the cruellest time for the band, or to be more precise, 4th December. For it was on this day in 1971 that the Montreux Casino burnt down during the Mothers Of Invention performance that the band was in attendance at. Although the fire was devastating, everyone managed to get out alive, but the Mothers' equipment was destroyed.

In the most well documented story in the band's entire history, it at least provided something positive - the inspiration for 'Smoke On The Water'. It proved to be a much worse time for Mothers' leader Frank Zappa who six days later during a show (with hired equipment) at London's Rainbow Theatre, encountered a member of the audience who ran up the side steps of the stage and pushed Zappa ten feet into the orchestra pit, knocking him unconscious and breaking his leg. It prompted Ian Gillan to sometimes throw in the spontaneous line 'break a leg Frank', which he did during the recording session a few days later. This wasn't included on the original release but did appear on the remixed version of *Machine Head* released in 1997. Gillan also subsequently sung the line at some gigs, such as the Paris Theatre, London, which was recorded for the *BBC In Concert* radio program that was also later released on disc.

On 4 December in 1975 a much darker and tragic event occurred in Jakarta, Indonesia. Following the band's first ever show in that country, one of their bodyguards, Patsy Collins, lost his life after falling down a lift shaft. Glenn Hughes and the band's road manager Rob Cooksey were arrested on suspicion of murder but later released without charge.

On 4 December the following year, with the band having officially announced its split in July, whilst on an American tour with his own band, Tommy Bolin died of a drug overdose in his Miami hotel room, aged 25. That wasn't the end of the tragedies for on 4 December, and as if to come full circle, Frank Zappa died of prostate cancer at his home in Los Angeles in 1993.

Another curious fact for 4 December is that although Deep Purple performed shows on that day in 1969 and 1970, following the '71 incident, on each subsequent occasion when the band toured in December there wasn't a show on that date for 35 years, with the exception of the ill-fated Indonesian gig. On the 1972 US tour, they had gigs on the 2nd and 3rd, then again on the 7th. On the 1974 US tour, a gig on the 3rd and one on the 5th.

Even when the band reformed, in 1984, during that debut reunion tour they played in New Zealand on the 2nd, and the next show was in Australia on the 5th. When they returned to Montreux for the *The House of Blue Light* album press launch in December 1986, the start of the three-day event avoided the 4th by four days, by kicking off on the 8th.

In 1993, following Blackmore's departure, Joe Satriani was drafted in to help the band complete the six-date Japan tour in December. Starting on the 2nd, they played every night through to the 8th, except the 4th! By the time that Steve Morse had taken over as Blackmore's permanent replacement the band once again toured North America in 1996. They played shows on the 1st and 2nd December, and again on the 5th and 6th. The following year, they started another US tour on the 5th December!

The band didn't tour in December again until 2003, this time in Europe, with shows in Poland and Germany on 2nd and 3rd, and then unsurprisingly a day off before the tour continued in Slovenia on the 5th!

A South American tour in 2006 that started in November went through to December with shows on 1st, 2nd and 3rd, 5th, 7th and 9th. And again, back in Europe in 2009 with December shows on 1st, 2nd and 3rd, 5th, 6th, 7th and 8th, but once again, not the 4th.

If it was a hoodoo of some sort, then the jinx was finally broken in 2010 when the band played at Le Cube Parc des Expos, Troyes, France. This was the first gig on 4 December since that ill-fated day in Jakarta 35 years earlier! Having gotten over the hurdle, the band next played on 4 December in 2012, this time at the Ziggodome in Amsterdam.

Football On The Water

In Jon Lord's hometown Leicester, for a number of years now the Tigers, one of England's most successful Rugby Football Union teams run on to the pitch at each home game to 'Smoke On The Water'. It was apparently initially played at the request of the team's (and England's) then captain Martin Johnson, as a good motivational piece of music - he liked it and it seemed to work for the team, and has become the norm at the Leicester Tigers Welford Road ground ever since.

Another rugby link comes in the shape of Richie Blackmore (born 2nd July 1969 in New Zealand) a Rugby Football League coach and former professional player who represented his country. On 19 November 1999, on the UK TV comedy/sports quiz show *They Think It's All Over*, one of the rounds involved giving clues to identify different sports stars that had a famous namesake in a different profession. Comedian Phil Jupitus' clue to his teammates; former cricketer David Gower, and athlete Roger Black was quite simply, "Rugby player and guitarist with Deep Purple". Even after he

gave a rendition of 'Smoke On The Water' they still didn't guess who it was! Clearly not fans!

There was also an Association football (soccer) goalkeeper called Richie Blackmore who started as an apprentice with Bristol City, the same year that Deep Purple started! He then joined Walsall, followed by Birmingham City, where he signed professionally, and later played for many years in the Irish League for Dundalk and Galway.

Another interesting fact and coincidence about this particular Richie Blackmore is that in 1972 he moved to the USA to join New York Cosmos. Cosmos was owned by Purple's US record company, Warner Bros, and played their home matches at the University Ground at Hofstra - the very same University where Deep Purple performed the following year, for a show filmed by ABC TV and now available on the DVD *Live in Concert 1972/73*! You couldn't make it up!

Notable fans

As one would expect Deep Purple has a huge fan base around the world. Today with social media, the official *Facebook* page has around 4 million followers, but long before the Internet existed Deep Purple had several notable fans.

In 1970 Manchester United and Northern Ireland footballer George Best was just about one of the most famous people in Britain. He can be seen watching the band's TV show *Doing Their Thing* filmed for Granada TV at it's Manchester studios in August. He later built up a friendship with Ian Gillan and appeared in Gillan's career documentary film *Highway Star*. BBC Radio 1 disc jockey Dave Lee Travis was amongst the crowd at the Royal Albert Hall for the premiere of the *Concerto For Group & Orchestra* and can be clearly seen in the film that was produced and originally broadcasted on the BBC in early 1970. That same year, and as previously documented earlier in this tome (see page 40) the man who was Britain's Prime Minister between 1997 and 2010 is a major fan. Also from the world of politics, Russia's former President and current Prime Minister Medvedev is a massive Purple fan. In 2007 he said, "I can boast that I have the entire Deep Purple collection."He attended a show they performed at the Kremlin in 2008 and met the band at the concert.

As also documented on page 79 it can't be confirmed that he is actually a fan, but certainly John Bercow, the speaker of the UK's House of Commons is switched on enough to refer to them when discussing the behaviour of members of parliament.

From the world of sport, tennis player and TV commentator Boris Becker is the proud owner of a choice piece of Purple memorabilia. Becker made sporting history when he became the youngest ever winner of Wimbledon in 1985. Following his victory when he returned to his hometown of Leimen of 12 July, more than 15,000 gathered along the road to welcome home the youngest, the first unseeded, and the first West German player to win at Wimbledon.

On the town hall's balcony, Becker graciously received the official certificate and gold "Ring of Honour" presented to him by the Mayor, but he was more pleased by Deep Purple's gift of a gold record for the band's reunion album *Perfect Strangers* released in September the previous year.

Another German sports star who is a fan is footballer, Lothar Matthäus, who met Ritchie Blackmore during the band's 1988 Italian tour. He was playing for Inter Milan at the time. Another notable footballer, Manchester United and Denmark goalkeeper Peter Schmeichel paid £2,000 for a Fender *Stratocaster* signed by Ritchie Blackmore in a Nordoff-Robins charity auction in 1999. Formula 1 driver Sebastian Vettel is one of several quoted in the booklet that accompanied the 40th anniversary *Machine Head* box set. As was fellow Formula 1 Irishman Eddie Jordan who met the band when they played a show at the F1 race track in Melbourne in 2001.

Australian entertainer Tim Minchin has the honour of being the first fan to pick a Deep Purple track when he appeared on the long-running BBC Radio 4 series *Desert Island Discs*. He elected an inspired and unpredictable choice of the single B-side 'I'm Alone'. Dame Wendy Hall, is the second person to date to pick a Purple song on the same show, with the much more predictable 'Smoke On The Water'.

The Australian environmental campaigner Jon Dee, a successful charity fundraiser and rock fan went one step further following the Spitak earthquake which struck Armenia, killing 25,000 people on 7 December 1988. He started using his charity contacts in the Soviet nation to get horrific television footage of the disaster to Western networks. "I found myself just watching hours and hours of this raw footage, things too horrible to put into words or to show on television," Dee said. "The images stayed with me."

He then had an idea to ring around his friends in the hard-rock community including Ian Gillan, along with Brian May of Queen, David Gilmour of Pink Floyd and the tennis players Pat Cash and John McEnroe. A few months later many musicians gathered in Metropolis Studios in Chiswick, London to record a version of 'Smoke On The Water', which Ritchie Blackmore also added his licks to, after the others had left the studio.

It culminated in Rock Aid Armenia, the biggest charity rock album since Live Aid and a top 40 hit in Britain, with all the proceeds helping the tens of thousands of people affected by the quake.

Tennis star, Pat Cash became involved in the project in 1988 when he was on the world tennis circuit and later contributed to a recording of Led Zeppelin's 'Rock and Roll' as a lead guitarist along with fellow tennis star John McEnroe, Roger Daltrey, and Steve Harris and Nicko McBrain from Iron Maiden. The author met Pat Cash at Purple's show at Hammersmith, 15 November 2009, and he graciously supplies the foreword to this book.

Needless to say, from the world of rock music, Deep Purple has many fans amongst their fellow musicians. Metallica's Lars Ulrich is probably the most avid champion of the band, and has appeared in several documentaries singing the praises of the group he first saw in 1973 in his native Denmark. Fellow Scandinavians, in the shape of Swedish band Opeth, went as far as doing a pastiche of the *Concerto For Group & Orchestra* cover for their *In Live Concert At The Royal Albert Hall* album in honour of Purple.

Iron Maiden front man Bruce Dickinson was first introduced to rock after hearing 'Child in Time' being played in another student's room. It resulted in his first album purchase *In Rock*, which created his interest in rock music, and of course since then has not only sung Purple's praises at every opportunity but has also performed with them and various band members at charity concerts, as well as providing some of the vocals for Lord's studio recording of *Concerto For Group & Orchestra* in 2011.

As mentioned on page 80 Def Leppard guitarist Phil Collen also saw the band during his teenage years. UK Indie band Kula Shaker had a big hit with 'Hush' in 1998, and frontman Crispian Mills is not only a fan but even sported a cool Deep Purple t-shirt during a TV performance. Bryan Adams is also a huge fan and despite being a competent guitarist once commented on Blackmore's skills by saying "no matter how much I practice, I'm still not worthy."

One musician who initially is a less obvious fan is Joy Division/New Order bassist Peter Hook. Whilst on a BBC TV show presented by Danny Baker he said: "I did like Deep Purple I must admit. I suppose it's one of those interesting things as you get older and hopefully a little bit wiser you try and move on but can't. With Deep Purple musically they did have subtlety. They had different moods throughout an album. I must admit it was one frightening thing when we got back together again as New Order in 2001-2. We did a French festival and Deep Purple was on before us. Barney and I were laughing, going 'Deep Purple, oh man this is going to be a cake walk' and oh my god to go on after them, they were fantastic. They blew us off. It was the only time I've actually been scared to go on stage because it was after Deep Purple. That was an unbelievable night. They played so well."

As a side to this, and another interesting fact. Given Hook's love of Deep Purple it may fascinate you to know that some of New Order's earliest gigs were actually shorter than some of Deep Purple's live performances of 'Mandrake Root' and 'Wring That Neck'!

And last but not least, arguably Deep Purple's number one fan has to be Ian Gillan. His favourite line-up? MkII? The period with Joe Satriani? Or the current line-up with Steve Morse and Don Airey? Well, I'll let Ian explain: "I was a fan of the band before I joined, so my favourite was the one with Rod Evans and Nick Simper. Those albums were absolutely fantastic. I played them to death before I got the gig. Obviously the first incarnation when I joined was extremely special because of the innovations that came in at the time. The camaraderie was brilliant."

Smoke On The Water

Since 'Smoke On The Water' was originally recorded in Montreux in December 1971, there has now been in excess of 40 different versions officially released on a plethora of live albums. And that is before counting all the versions also released by the band members solo output, such as the Ian Gillan Band, and Rainbow.

Although several Purple numbers have been acknowledged as being influenced by other songs, it's less well documented that the riff for "Smoke" is taken from a Bossa Nova song 'Maria Quiet', written by Carlos Lyra and Norman Gimbel and performed by Brazilian singer Astrud Gilberto of 'Girl From Ipanema' fame. 'Maria Quiet' is a track, which also somewhat prophetically is from her 1966 LP *Look To The Rainbow*, produced by Gil Evans.

Not surprisingly 'Smoke On The Water' has also seen the most extensive number of interpretations of all Purple's songs. Including many quite bizarre adaptations such as Canadian Nash The Slash and his version entitled 'Dopes On The Water'. And we must not forget to mention Pat Boone's version, from his covers album of well-known rock songs *In A Metal Mood*. Complete with brass section, it was given a big band-cum-Latin feel to it, which is interesting as the arranger felt the tune lent itself to that type of arrangement. Perhaps subconsciously he was thinking of the Gilberto tune?

Frank Zappa's son Dweezil was drafted in to play guitar, but much more interesting was Blackmore's involvement, playing the solo, and fully complimenting the feel of the arrangement, sounding more like Carlos Santana than Ritchie Blackmore! He did it for his Dad, who was a Pat Boone fan!

Ten years on, Don Airey plays Purple classic for the first time

Deep Purple's keyboard player since 2002 has had a long and illustrious career that has included working with the likes of Black Sabbath, Whitesnake and Jethro Tull. He was of course also in Blackmore's Rainbow in the early eighties. Over his career he has performed with countless others and played on numerous songs.

On 30 August 2012 along with his own band, that perform as Don Airey and Friends, he was playing a warm-up show in his local pub, the Crown and Cushion, prior to a European tour. The band's regular guitarist Rob Harris couldn't make it due to his other commitments with Jamiroquai. His stand-in was Howie G who stepped in at short notice, with virtually no rehearsing. As a result they had to change the set and drop some of the band's regular numbers and replace them with material that Howie G was familiar with. Amongst these was the Deep Purple classic 'Mistreated'. After the show Airey informed the author that it was the first time he had ever performed it. As this was a joint Blackmore/Coverdale composition it clearly would never get performed at a current Deep Purple show fronted by Ian Gillan. And even though Blackmore played it in the early years of Rainbow he had dropped it from the show just at the point when Airey joined. It was played by Rainbow as an audition number for Graham Bonnet in early 1979, but it is unclear whether or not Airey was merely an observer or not. Even if it had escaped his memory of playing it back then, it was certainly the first time Purple's keyboard player had played 'Mistreated' in a live environment.

Another little-known Don Airey fact is that when he isn't performing with Purple or his own band he often joins local jazz musicians in pubs playing jazz standards.

Ian lasts the Paice

Although drummer Ian Paice has been the only constant throughout the band's entire career, he does not appear on every song the band has recorded. 'This Time Around' from the 1975 *Come Taste The Band* album was a joint Glenn Hughes and Jon Lord collaboration, which was only performed by the duo.

But that aside, not only is drumming the most physically demanding of all rock's instruments, but Paice's longevity is made even more astonishing because since childhood he has lived with only one fully functional lung, making his feat even more incredible.

Unlike many rock drummers Paicey doesn't use a double bass drum set up and in the early days of Purple he produced those astonishing solos with a tiny kit consisting of only five drums. There was however one exception to the double bass drum set up. He used it for 'Fireball' and when they played it as an encore for a brief period in late '71 and early '72, the roadies set up a second bass drum, solely for that number. But strangely when it was brought back in to the set in 1996 he did the same song using one bass drum!

The most notable characteristic of Paice's drum style is his swing, which is all as a result of his upbringing. "I was born in Nottingham, and when I was sort of 3, nearly 4 years old my father's job took him to Germany and we lived in Germany for 3 years - Berlin and Cologne. Then we came back and we lived just outside Oxford, a little town called Bicester. My father was a civil servant and he was working in an Army Ordinance depot. He was a piano player, a very, very good one. Before the war, he was as close to professional as you could get in Britain in those days. And he still used to do weekend gigs with a trio or a quartet, playing dance music for people having dinner in hotels. And occasionally his drummer wouldn't be available."

"I started beating the furniture up when I was about 12 years old with a pair of mum's knitting needles. I was watching old movies on the telly and trying to copy what the drummers were doing. And when I was 15 he got me my first awful little kit, They looked like drums but that was as close as they got to it. But occasionally he would ask me to do the gig when his main guy couldn't do it. And that's how I started playing, waltzes and quicksteps and foxtrots, and learning when to shut up, when to make a noise and when to push things and when to just back up into... And although it was a little dull it was invaluable musically to learn your position in any piece of music, and when you do something, when you don't do anything. So I did that for 3 or 4 months, so I suppose I played with him, I don't know, 13 or 14 times, something like that. The good thing is I used to get as much money from him for a Saturday night as I used to get for 3 days at work."

"I was lucky, because my musical spectrum was really varied, and that came through my father. Obviously all the records we had were his stuff; they were big band swing, piano trios, classical, you know. What we didn't have in my house, we never had any blues records, we never had any folk/country records, but I had the jazz and I had the classical thing. So when I started playing rock 'n roll sometimes the only way I could feel something was with this jazz swing."

"The jazz stuff gave me a different way of playing rock 'n roll because I couldn't do it the way all the other kids do it, I couldn't play it straight up and down, it had to have a little bounce, it had to have some syncopation. And that has made what I've done slightly different and for good or bad reasons, made people notice what I do. It definitely made Ritchie notice, which gave me the break to be asked to join Deep Purple."

Often referred to as the Guv'ner, Little Ian's career has also included time with Paice Ashton Lord, Whitesnake, Gary Moore, and sessions for a host of top names including Paul McCartney and George Harrison (see page 130). His outside interests include sea fishing and horse racing. Paicey has owned several racehorses over the years, including one called Perfect Stranger. In recent years when Purple has taken time off from touring, he has often spent it performing with Deep Purple tribute bands!

In 2013 he was acknowledged in a somewhat unexpected fashion when Nottingham's *Castle Rock Brewery* produced beers to celebrate famous folks born in the city. A limited edition "Ian Paice Nottinghamian Celebration Ale" was sold in local pubs.

Rarest Record

When it comes to rare records, more often than not, rarity value is often linked to financial value. However some of the rarest Deep Purple records were only pressed in quantities of a few hundred, yet the collector value remains quite low. Chief amongst these are the promotional interview LPs that were released for the 1984

Perfect Strangers and 1987 *The House of Blue Light* albums and fetch around £15-20 ($30). The latter, it is thought, was only produced in a quantity of 300. Although essentially an interview with Gillan, Glover, Lord and Paice, it does finish with a little bit of ad-lib music by Lord and Paice, which they call 'The Frank Sonata'.

Rarities continue to be produced for new releases such as the 11-disc white label test pressings for the vinyl editions of the remixed *Made In Japan* box set released in May 2014. It contained the 9LP set comprising the three concerts in full, and the 2LP set of the original album remixed. Only ten copies were pressed up in this format, easily making it one of the rarest Deep Purple items of all.

But it's a combination of scarcity and desirability that are the key ingredients to also making the rarest records the most valuable, and most of these stem from the earliest part of the band's career. Particularly desirable are the Japanese singles released by the first line-up, all of which came in picture sleeves, something that was a far less common occurrence in the UK and USA at that time. These have been known to sell for several hundreds of pounds each. The Japanese also produced a couple of compilation albums of MKI material in 1970, one of which was a double LP, with 2

sides featuring Jimi Hendrix and entitled *Battle Of Deep Purple & Jimi Hendrix*. It came in a round film-type metal canister.

Also sought after are the UK and US promos for the debut single 'Hush'. Whilst this song went on to sell around a million copies in the US and made number four on the *Billboard* chart, promo copies, which came in a picture sleeve and were sent out to radio stations and record stores, are much sought after.

Those early releases were issued in America on the *Tetragrammaton* label, which was founded in 1968 by artist entertainment manager Roy Silver, Bruce Post Campbell, Marvin Deane, and comedian Bill Cosby (whose manager was Roy Silver). Unfortunately the company's lavish spending soon caught up with them, but it did result in one of the rarest of all Deep Purple records. In December 1969 *Tetragrammaton* released *Concerto For Group & Orchestra*, a few weeks ahead of other territories, but within months the company had called in the administrators and production ceased. Deep Purple's popularity was already on the wane, following the previous year's success. *Concerto For Group & Orchestra* was the last release on the label, and although it is not known just how many copies were pressed up, the fact that it was only in production for a few weeks, makes this undoubtedly one of the hardest variations of a Deep Purple record to find. Likewise the Japanese promo releases of both this album and *In Rock* in red vinyl are also extremely rare and are two of the most desirable Deep Purple collectibles.

An oddity from more recent times involves the *Live in Europe 1993* box set. BMG started sending out review copies until they realised the discs were labelled up wrongly with the discs for the Birmingham show actually playing Stuttgart and vice versa. Apparently only about 25 misspressed copies were sent out before BMG realised the error. The rest of the batch was destroyed and an entirely new batch produced, making these oddities one of the rarest Deep Purple items to date!

But as rare as these are, the accolade of Deep Purple's rarest record is without doubt the first recording made under the name of Roundabout. It was recorded at Trident Studios in April 1968. In fact the management had booked the studio time even before they had found their singer. Nick Simper recalls that both Paice and Evans had only been in the band a few days by the time of the session. They cut four songs: two covers, 'Hush' and 'Help!', and two original numbers, 'Love Help Me' and 'Shadows'. The latter two were then pressed up as an acetate in order to interest prospective labels. Simper also recalls that along with Evans and Lord they returned to the studio to lay down the vocals for 'Love Help Me', just before they set off to Denmark for their first gigs. However for some unexplained reason during the transfer, the vocal track was accidentally excluded. However it was on the strength of this recording that *Tetragrammaton* signed the band. Unlike normal vinyl, which is quickly formed from lumps of plastic by a mass-production moulding process, a so-called acetate disc is created by using a recording lathe to cut a sound-modulated groove into the surface of a special lacquer-coated blank disc. And although they can be played on any normal record player they are degraded by wear much more quickly than vinyl.

Because of the nature of the way there are produced, acetates are always pressed up in very small quantities. As an example, in 1958 an acetate was made of two songs by The Quarrymen, featuring John Lennon, Paul McCartney and George Harrison. After being thought lost it was found in 1981 and sold to Paul McCartney for an undisclosed fee.

There were certainly more than one copy of the Roundabout acetate made. The exact quantity is not certain but Nick Simper reckons about six copies were pressed up and only 4 are thought to have survived. Whatever the exact quantity was, it is certainly the rarest Deep Purple record by far. Out of interest, Simper sold his personal copy back in the nineties to an Italian collector. Both tracks were dubbed from the acetate and released for the first time in 1985 on the *Anthology* compilation album. They were also included on the remastered *Shades of Deep Purple* release in 2000 and the *Hard Road* box set in 2014.

Did You Know...

* When the band was originally formed, several names were suggested including Concrete God and Orpheus.

* *Shades of Deep Purple* has been released in the UK on vinyl no less than six times: Parlophone mono edition (PMC 7055) 1968; Parlophone stereo edition (PCS 7055) 1968; Harvest Heritage edition (SHSM 2016) 1977; Harvest Heritage edition (SHSM 2016) with sleeve design of abandoned car with a doll on it - rejected 1977 artwork printed in error and quickly withdrawn 1987; Parlophone EMI 100th anniversary, virgin vinyl 180g pressing edition (LPCENT 25) 1997 and Parlophone mono, purple vinyl limited edition (PMCR 7055), 2014.

* Deep Purple did a live concert in the afternoon from Birmingham Top Rank Suite on 6th February 1969 for the BBC *Radio 1 Club*. The show ran from midday to 2:00 but alas is thought not to exist anymore. Many live broadcasts weren't even recorded by the BBC! The Move were also on the show and were impressed with the clothes Purple wore, particularly Rod Evans's 'chainmail' vest he had bought in California!

* Despite the *Concerto For Group & Orchestra* featuring only three lengthy movements, both Harvest and Warner Brothers released singles from it! Albeit for promotional use only. The Harvest one had brief extracts from the first and second movements and the Warners' one, the same sixty second extract on both sides.

* 'Flight Of The Rat' was released as a single in New Zealand, with 'And The Address' on the b-side. In 2009 it was used in the soundtrack for *The Damned United*.

* When Purple Records was set up in late 1971 for Europe, future releases all appeared on that label except in Greece where the albums continued to appear on Harvest Records, right through to, and including *Come Taste The Band*.

* During 'Lucille' in the Copenhagen 1972 concert film Ritchie Blackmore briefly does the Chuck Berry duck walk!

* When the concert was released on DVD as *Live in Concert 1972/73*, the initial batch of promo discs that EMI sent out actually contained a live concert video of The Shadows!

* The live 20-minute version of 'Space Truckin'' from *Made In Japan* was released as a 7" single in Mexico! It was split over both sides at 33 ⅓rpm.

* During MKIII's four warm-up gigs in December 1973, 'What's Goin' On Here' was played as an encore. It's the only time the band has ever played it in concert.

* After the show at the Festhalle, Berne, Switzerland on 29 September 1974 Blackmore played another show at the Babalu Club with the Sensational Alex Harvey Band... on bass!

* The cover of a later re-print of the 1971 novel *Song Of The Scorpions* by Paul Tabori included an artist's impression of a photo of Tommy Bolin with a moustache added!

* Although not credited on the sleeve, Tommy Bolin played the bass on 'Comin' Home' from *Come Taste The Band*. It was the last song recorded for the album and Glenn Hughes had been sent home to recuperate following a drug-induced meltdown.

* *Last Concert In Japan* was never officially released in the UK but a catalogue number (TPS 3514) was issued for it and used on the Australian release, which printed on the label; "first published © ℗ 1978 in U.K."

* When *Perfect Strangers* was released on 29 October 1984 it was the first Deep Purple album to be released on compact disc.

* Having lost out to Polydor in signing the reformed MKII, EMI UK released a double LP *Anthology* from the '68-76 era in February 1985. Later in the year they took to reissuing *In Rock*, *Fireball* and *Machine Head* as picture disc LPs with posters. They also released four 3-track 12" singles. If you bought all four and sent the sleeve stickers to EMI you received a free 7" single 'Smoke On My Mega Mix' coupled with 'Mixed Alive'. Both tracks contained brief clips of several tracks re-mixed as medleys!

* Both Paris shows in 1985 were filmed, and the second night has been broadcast several times on WDR TV. But Ian Gillan was suffering from a cold, and the management don't want it released although 'A Gypsy's Kiss' was

included on the *New Live & Rare: The Video Collection 1984-2000* compilation DVD. Blackmore, Glover and Gillan did the Shadows dance routine during 'Black Night'. The first night's show was blighted by Lord's organ failing during 'Space Truckin'' and he had to complete the show on piano.

* At the gig in Cologne on 8 February 1987 Jon Lord had a toilet seat hanging from his Hammond organ!

* The running order for Slaves And Masters is different on the CD and vinyl versions. The first 3 tracks are the same on both, as is track 6 and tracks 8 and 9, but on the CD tracks 4, 5 and 7 are: 'Truth Hurts', 'Breakfast In Bed', and 'Fortuneteller, whilst on the LP they are 'Fortuneteller', 'Truth Hurts' and 'Breakfast In Bed'.

* 'Too Much Is Not Enough' was a song Joe Lynn Turner had written with Bob Held and Al Greenwood for a solo album, before it was decided to include it on *Slaves And Masters*. The following year Paul Rodgers recorded a version of it with Kenney Jones, with their then band The Law, but did not release it.

* 'Wicked Ways' was only performed at the first few shows of the 1991 tour, and was soon dropped from the set, but it was in the first show in Ostrava, Czechoslovakia, on 4th February that was filmed and broadcasted on Czech TV.

* During the show in Denmark on 6 March 1991, the band broke into 'Fortuneteller' at the end of 'Truth Hurts' but it was never performed in its entirety.

* In the early nineties when Musicland Studios in Munich closed down they discovered the master tapes for *Stormbringer* and *Come Taste The Band* and almost threw them away. But Reinhold Mack, the studio's engineer returned them to Thames Talent, the band's current management. However they are the property of Deep Purple (Overseas) Ltd, the company overseen by the band's original management HEC Enterprises, and eventually they were returned to their rightful owner and are currently stored at Abbey Road.

* The backing tracks for *The Battle Rages On* were recorded at Bearsville Studios in New York State. The studio was created by Albert Grossman; manager of Bob Dylan and The Band. 'Chest Fever' from The Band's debut album *Music From Big Pink* was Jon Lord's inspiration for 'Might Just Take Your Life'. The Lowry organ that Garth Hudson had played on 'Chest Fever' was still in the studio when they recorded *The Battle Rages On*. Lord used a Hammond B-3 found in the studio that he thought was probably Hudson's.

DEEP HATRED!

ROCK legends Deep Purple are a band at war . . . and this picture is a perfect illustration of it.

The heavy metal veterans have just released a ~~...~~ es On. Trouble is, the

Purple pic a quarrel

~~...~~re failed to make an inter- ~~...~~ last month because of ~~...~~lth, Gillan quipped: ~~...~~morrhoids— ~~...~~t he's a

The Battle Rages On

DEEP PURPLE

25th Anniversary

* When the MKII line-up reunited in 1992, they refused to do a video or any p o s s i b l e promotion for the album, and even denied photographers a group session. All the press got was a jigsaw with cartoon drawings of the group!

Manchester Apollo, 5 November 1993. One of only 37 dates the MKII line-up completed during the final tour played under a somewhat fraught atmosphere.

* The 1998 25th anniversary CD remaster of *Made In Japan* included a bonus disc with three encore numbers of 'Black Night', 'Speed King' and 'Lucille'. However, the Spanish edition filled the disc up by including the studio recordings of the seven original *Made In Japan* tracks.

* Prior to joining Deep Purple full time in 2002, Don Airey was called upon to do some gigs at short notice the previous year when Jon Lord sustained an injury. The day before Don got the call he was in a record shop and purchased *Fireball* & *In Rock*. "I just sat at home & played them all day, thinking how wonderful it was. Very odd!"

* An episode of the BBC's highbrow *Mastermind* quiz screened on 4th August 2003 included a contestant who's chosen specialist subject was Deep Purple. One question asked was "when Ian Gillan left the group in June 1973, which former Marbles vocalist was his temporary replacement before David Coverdale joined?" Not surprisingly he didn't know the answer as the question was incorrect to start with! But compere, John Humphries gave the answer as Graham Bonnet!

* Nobody's gonna take my car... One of the most recognisable lines from 'Highway Star' might well have remained true through the years, however, whilst Ian Gillan may have kept his car, he was banned from driving it in 2004. Gillan, then 58, was seen walking unsteadily to his car near his home in Lyme Regis, Dorset, shortly after midnight on 22nd May. Police stopped him after he left the Cobb Gate car park and he was found to have 76 micrograms of alcohol in 100 millilitres of breath; more than twice the legal limit of 35 micrograms. At the court hearing he pleaded guilty and was fined £500 with £50 costs. Weymouth magistrates also banned him from driving for 16 months. For a while it meant Ian was less of a highway star and more of a footpath  star! Published on the Internet, but not substantiated are claims that Rod Evans was arrested for driving under influence in California the same year!

* The *BBC Sessions 1968–1970* release of 2011 did not include every session because the tapes for some of them are thought to no longer exist. However the *Top of the Pops* version of 'Black Night' does exist and was omitted. In those days, due to Musicians Union rules the bands were not allowed to mime to the record but had to record it again at the BBC, then mime to the new recording!

* The 2006 BBC1 TV drama series *Life On Mars* based in 1973 used as part of its soundtrack in the first episode (9th Jan), 'Rat Bat Blue' and 'Fireball'. In the scene where 'Fireball' was playing, the record on the turntable wasn't correct as it wasn't the Harvest label, but an eighties Epic one.

* The Japanese DVD Version of *Perfect Strangers Live* recorded in Sydney on 12th December has a bonus track of 'Highway Star' from the following night's gig, (where George Harrison appeared for the encore 'Lucille'). All three Sydney nights were professionally filmed.

Purple play illegal gigs!

In 2011, Roger Glover became a father again at the ripe old age of 65. As Glover wanted to be present at the birth it meant he had to bale out of a handful of gigs booked for Cyprus, Greece, Israel and Turkey in May of that year.

He missed nine shows in all with his place being taken by former Jamirouquai bassist Nick Fyffe. Fyffe was known to the band as he had previously played on some of Jon Lord's solo work, as well as regularly appearing at the annual *Sunflower Jam* charity gig organised by Ian Paice's wife Jackie.

However, Glover's absence technically meant that for those shows the band should not have called itself Deep Purple. This was kick-started by the ruling made in 1980 following Rod Evans single-handed Deep Purple "reunion" (see page 115). After Evans had been sued in the courts for using the name, it was agreed and written in law that any future incarnation of the band must include at least three of seven members who at the time were all still linked with the original Deep Purple management organisation, HEC Enterprises.

When the band reformed in 1984, instead of being managed by HEC they chose Thames Talent, the company operated by their former US booking agent and Rainbow's manager, Bruce Payne. Although HEC had the rights to the name, around 1987 it granted Thames Talent permission to use it subject to the band including three of the seven, as outlined during the Evan's case.

Although it was highly unlikely that anyone was ever going to challenge that they should not be called Deep Purple with Nick Fyffe on bass, they were technically in breach of the agreement and therefore illegal!

Had the band thought about this at the time and wanted to be certain of not falling foul of the law, even if they had asked original bassist Nick Simper to act as Glover's temporary stand-in, that would still have been illegal.

Simper had signed away his rights years earlier and is not one of the seven in question. The seven were: Blackmore, Lord, Paice, Glover, Gillan, Coverdale & Hughes.

So to keep on the right side of the law, Glenn Hughes could have stood in, or indeed David Coverdale although it is unclear as to how good his bass guitar skills are! Perhaps he could have played bass pedals, or Jon Lord could have played bass notes on the organ?

The band found itself in a similar situation again, on July 14 2013 at the Kunstrasen in Bonn, Germany when Glover was not feeling well and Fyffe stepped in again. If someone actually reminds them of the ruling, then it looks as if Glenn Hughes would have to be called in next time. Or even more fascinating, they could ask Blackmore, who is also quite adept on bass guitar. Now that is something to ponder, and to conclude this book with - Deep Purple featuring Steve Morse on lead and Ritchie Blackmore on bass!

Acknowledgements

Don Airey, Marco Armari, Lynn Baker, Ritchie Blackmore, Tony Carey, Raymond D'addario, Deep Purple (Overseas) Ltd, Mike DiMeo, Kevin Dixon, EMI Records, Micke Eriksson, Rob Fodder, Pericle Formenti, Helmut Gerlach, Tarquin Gotch, Roger Glover, Ian Hansford, Colin Hart, Rasmus Heide, Dec Hickey, Glenn Hughes, Neil Jeffries, Gerhard Koritnik, Hartmut Kreckel, Bernt Küpper, Dave Lewis, Jon Lord, Christian Meyer zu Natrup, Steve Morse, Simon Robinson, Nick Simper, Carole Stevens, Alan Stutz, Drew Thompson, Joe Lynn Turner, Universal Records, Lisa Walker, Nick Warburton, Mike Wheeler, Alan Whitman and Nigel Young.

Bibliography

Papers
New Musical Express
Melody Maker
Sounds
Billboard
Bedfordshire Times
Bedford Record
Bedford Journal
New Haven Register
Mail On Sunday

Magazines
Disc And Music Echo 1969-72
Beat International 1969-73
Guitar Player 1973
Stargazer, *DPAS Publication 1975-84*
Darker Than Blue *DPAS publication 1984-2012*
Deep Purple Forever *Eriksson, 1991-2002*
More Black than Purple *Welch, Mark/Bloom, Jerry, MBTP/Wymer 1996-2014*
Record Collector *Diamond Publishing Ltd, December 2004*
Classic Rock *Future, 2011*

Books
Guinness Book of Records *McWhirter, Ross & Norris, Guinness, 1973*
Deep Purple Illustrated Biography *Charlesworth, Chris, Omnibus 1983*
Black Knight *Bloom, Jerry, Omnibus 2005*
The More Black than Purple Interviews *Bloom, Jerry, Wymer 2007*
A Hart Life *Hart, Colin / Allix, Dick, Wymer 2011*
Hell Ain't A Bad Place To Be *Wall, Mick, Orion 2012*

Internet & Radio
BBC Radio 1, Friday Rock Show, 21 June 1985
3DB Radio, Melbourne, 21 November 1976
Internet Movie Database (imdb.com)
Telegraph.co.uk
www.blabbermouth.net/news/
www.45cat.com
www.discogs.com
www.ukrockfestivals.com

About The Author

Jerry Bloom first heard Deep Purple in 1971 but wasn't truly bitten by the bug until 1976 when he heard *Made in Europe*. The extra punch that the live recording gave to the music, particularly to the guitar and organ sold him on their unique brand of rock, and from that point on there was no looking back. He has seen Purple in concert over 30 times and has attended more than 100 shows of the various individual band members.

His passion eventually led to co-founding the Ritchie Blackmore magazine *More Black than Purple* in 1996, which he continued to edit up to 2014 when it was passed on to a new publisher and editor, Phil Syphe.

Since 1997 he has also done freelance writing for various record companies; in 1998 at the request of Blackmore's management he acted in an advisory capacity on the US 4 CD box set release, *Shades 1968–1998*; in 2003 he produced the official *Ghost of a Rose* tour programme for Blackmore's Night and in 2006 his first book, *Black Knight - the unauthorised Ritchie Blackmore Biography*, was published. That same year he instigated the release, and wrote the sleeve notes for SonyBMG's *Deep Purple Live In Europe 1993* box set. He also compiled the tracklisting for the same company's 3CD *Greatest Hits* compilation.

In 2008 he promoted a Deep Purple convention to celebrate the band's fortieth anniversary that included live performances from Nick Simper, (with his band the Good Old Boys), and Glenn Hughes. It brought together the two former Purple bassists for the first time ever. The Good Old Boys performance was released as *Live At The Deep Purple Convention* on his own company's record label the following year. It was followed up with another release by Simper - *The Deep Purple MKI Songbook* - new interpretations of early Purple songs, accompanied by the Austrian band Nasty Habits. A single – 'Roadhouse Blues' – was also released - Simper's first single release in over two decades.

In 2010 he started working for Glenn Hughes on his European solo tour, and on the first two Black Country Communion gigs. He was tour manager for both Hughes's 2011 UK electric and acoustic tours and his 2012 double bill dates with Fish.

He was also fortunate to be one of a handful of people to witness the last ever live performance by Jon Lord at St Andrew's Church in Nuthurst, Sussex, on 10 July 2011, as well as sharing a bottle of wine with the great man after the show. A moment he will treasure forevermore.

His other musical favourites are extremely eclectic, and include Free, Frank Zappa, Bob Dylan, The Band, J.S Bach, The Kinks, Slade, Abba, Muddy Waters, Genesis, The Stranglers, Edvard Grieg, Enya, The Cardigans and Mostly Autumn, whose fanzine he edited and published for a decade.

Outside of music he enjoys, cricket, rugby, football, cult British TV shows of the sixties and seventies such as *The Sweeney* and *The Professionals*, and visiting antique fairs and historic English buildings.

He also has a passion for *Jaguar* cars that goes back to the late sixties when he first had a ride in his uncle's S-Type.

Index

All albums, films, and books are in italics. Songs are in single quotation marks.

Also Available from Wymer

A Hart Life
(Colin Hart with Dick Allix)
*The life story of Deep Purple
and Rainbow's tour manager*

Forewords by Roger Glover & Paul Mann

"Colin was our mother hen" - Jon Lord

Colin Hart, the former Deep Purple and Rainbow tour manager devoted over thirty years of his life to these great rock musicians. This is his story and indeed theirs. A tale of excess in terms of greed, petulance, anger and devotion. It is counter balanced by extremes of pure talent, showmanship and, of course musicianship. He was the constant 'man in the middle' through all of the break ups, make-ups and revolving door line-up changes. Joining them at twenty-four years old and leaving with a curt email dismissal thirty years later, he was there every step of their rock 'n' roll way. A story of two of the most innovative, often copied, rock bands; seen through the eyes, ears and emotions of their 'mother hen'. He was their minder, chauffeur, carer, provider, protector, father confessor & confidant. In truth he is the only one who can tell this tale of both bands as he was the only one there on the road throughout the life of, not one, but both gigantic bands.

ISBN: 978-1-908724-04-5
Format: Paperback (234 x 156mm)
256pp (including 2 x 16 page b/w photo sections)

Zermattitis: A Musicians' Guide To Going Downhill Fast
(Tony Ashton)

Foreword by Jon Lord
Introduction by Sandra Ashton

Completed in 1991, Zermattitis, was the first of a planned trilogy of books written by the late Tony Ashton. Painstakingly transcribed from Tony's hand written manuscript, it is written in his inimitable style and will have your sides splitting with laughter throughout. Zermattitis isn't a straightforward autobiography, it's a collection of Tony's memoirs and short stories that starts with his love affair with Zermatt in Switzerland, which he first visited with Ashton Gardner & Dyke, and which gave him the title for the book. Other stories include his escapades on the road with many including Eric Clapton, George Harrison, Alice Cooper, Deep Purple and Paice Ashton Lord. Even the chapter on his bankruptcy is funnier than it has any right to be.

This limited edition hardback comes with a DVD of rare and previously unreleased Ashton Gardner & Dyke film featuring a live performance from Montreux Jazz Festival 1970, a rare promo film of The Ballad Of The Remo Four, Resurrection Shuffle TV broadcast, as well as Tony's performance of his homage to John Lennon, 'The Big Freedom Dance' filmed in part, in 1996, by Chris Evans.

Tony Ashton was one of the funniest and most life affirming people I have ever met. Above all he taught me one of life's great ways of staying sane and alive at the same time: Make a "V" sign, show you just don't care. Living by this advice has certainly done me no harm at all. For this alone I am truly grateful to Tony." **Billy Connolly**

"I loved Tony Ashton and his unique, slightly skewed, vision of the world. And here it is, in his own words, in this book." **Ewan McGregor**

ISBN: 978-0-9557542-9-6
Format: Hardback (234 x 156mm)
192pp plus DVD

Printed in October 2022
by Rotomail Italia S.p.A., Vignate (MI) - Italy